REVIVAL CRY

Contending For Transformation In This Generation

Trey Kent

ISBN: 1494471760
ISBN-13: 978-1494471767

UNCEASING PRAYER PUBLISHING
13427 Pond Springs Road
Austin, Texas 78729
All Scripture quotations taken from The Holy Bible, English Standard Version®
(ESV®) Copyright © 2001 by Crossway, a publishing ministry of Good News
Publishers. Used by permission of Crossway. All rights reserved. ESV Text
Edition: 2011. Italics in scriptural quotations indicate the author's added emphasis.

To Mary Anne,

the love of my life and my beautiful bride

CONTENTS

ACKNOWLEDGEMENTS

Why this book? I was sitting in the prayer room at Northwest Fellowship... Hold on. Before I tell you "Why this book", let me tell you that I began writing my first book a few months after I was saved in 1981. Fueled by my young and growing passion for God's Word, I decided that I should write a book to share my vast knowledge of God's Word. I pulled out my binder and began writing all I knew from Genesis to Revelation. After a page and a half of writing all I knew about the Bible, I decided it wasn't time to write my first book. But the seed was planted.

Thirty years later, while spending time in our church prayer room, God clearly and supernaturally called me to write this book. In a mere forty five seconds, He gave me the name *Revival Cry* and the outline for the first seven chapters. That was the easy part. During the past few years, I have labored with the amazing help of my best friend and wife, Mary Anne, to bring this book to you today. There's no way I could have done it without her! She's a keeper!

This book would not have been published without the publishing counsel of Eddie Clark, a wonderful friend and author. And you would not be holding this book or reading the electronic copy if it were not for the art and book design of Noe Banda. Also, special thanks to Andy Butcher for his expert work as editor. Thanks to all of Northwest Fellowship for the gracious gift of time you gave me to write this book. You are the best! I am forever grateful! I love you all!

Why this book? The answer is simple. God asked me to write it. This book was written to inspire regular believers like us to cry out and to see revival in our lifetime! I believe God has given me a message for the body of Christ for such a time as this.

Read it and let me know what you think.

Crying out for revival with you,

Trey Kent
Austin, Texas
December 10, 2013

RESPONSE TO REVIVAL CRY

"Trey Kent has written a world-class book on revival. Loaded with relevant quotes, powerful stories, excellent biblical exegesis, small group questions and helpful suggestions, the book is both a primer on revival and a call to pursue it in our lives. I welcome Trey's book and see it as an invaluable resource for those of us who are serious about seeking the outpouring of God's Spirit on our land."

Will Davis Jr
Senior Pastor, Austin Christian Fellowship

"There is a generation arising who will no longer live their lives according to the low standards of what western Christianity says is normal. Instead they will see how far they can go with their consecration, not because they are legalistic, but because they are ablaze with love for Jesus. With sincere passion and divine insight, my friend Trey Kent has laid out the blueprints of what this new normal looks like. If you long to see the complacency of your life shattered, if you long for your normal to look like the Bible and not like the world, then I urge you to read and apply the principles of Revival Cry to your life!"

Rick Pino
Fire Rain Ministries, Austin, TX

"Trey and Mary Anne Kent have a passion for prayer that is embodied in the church they lead. God is now using them along with others to lead a prayer movement in the churches of our city. This book portrays that passion for God's glory told with grace and humility."

Dan Davis
Founder of Hope Chapel and Pastors In Covenant Austin

"Many books have been written on the subject of revival but few have incorporated both the history of revival and the mystery of revival like Revival Cry. Pastor Trey Kent speaks from his heart and has skillfully woven a Biblical and historical picture of revival with an understanding of the individual believer's role in creating an atmosphere that is welcoming to the Holy Spirit's presence. This book is a necessary resource for those who want to be part of a revival generation."

Rick Randall
Senior Pastor, Austin Cornerstone Church

"Just when you have finished one of the best explanations of 2 Chron. 7:14, you are presented with three of the best chapters on the history of revival you will find anywhere."

Dr. David Smith
Executive Director, Austin Baptist Association

"In every major spiritual renewal in history, revival and prayer have gone hand in hand. Trey Kent is a man who lives that conviction, and I believe God has given him tremendous insight for our time. Our City is being transformed as I write these words, and God has used Trey as a critical instrument in this mighty work. Every passionate Christ follower should read this book!"

Ryan Rush
Senior Pastor, Bannockburn Baptist Church

"Wow! I just finished reading Revival Cry written by my good friend, Trey Kent, and I must say I am filled with overwhelming excitement and renewed hope for what God wants to do among us in these challenging times. Trey reminds us, in moving and compelling terms, about the compassionate heart of God and His willingness to send refreshment and revival – if we will simply ask Him! Trey has put in words what my heart longs for, but what I admit has grown sadly dim for me – like the last moments of a fading fire. But it's not just the words he writes that inspires me – rather it's the lifestyle Trey has chosen as an actual practitioner – a true man of prayer, even a giant among us – as an example of what God is calling all of us to be. I highly recommend Revival Cry to you to "fan into flame" what God desires to do among us when we seek Him in prayer! Lord, please send a Third Great Awakening in our day!"

Rob Harrell
Senior Pastor, First Evangelical Free Church

"Revival Cry captures the passion and priority of God's heart. Awakening His church to a love for Him which results in a dedication to making Him known in the Earth is the theme of this book and the lifestyle of it's author. Pastor Trey Kent does a masterful job of challenging the reader to consider a similar lifestyle, one that will live through the generations. Additionally, he details practical tools to cultivate and sustain a lifelong dedication to the passion and priority of God's heart. You will be challenged and equipped as you make your way through the pages of this book."

Charles Patterson
Founding Pastor, Church of the Hills, Austin, Texas

"The Kingdom moves upon the prayers and obedience of its saints. Revival Cry is both a prayer and study guide that will help you experience God anew. Revival is for the Body of Christ. The Word says, if we will but draw near to God will He not also draw near to us! Revival Cry is a solid primer for all saints to draw near to Him."

Dr. Rich Carney
Executive Director Austin Bridge Builders Alliance (ABBA)

Trey Kent

CHAPTER 1

YOUR MOST IMPORTANT IDENTITY: A HOUSE OF PRAYER

"If my people..."
- 2 Chronicles 7:14

Jesus. Love. Revival. These three words describe the greatest need of the church today. Thinking we are going to change our cities by growing our churches is false. We need revival. We need churches on fire. True change begins with Jesus, with being consumed with Him. Jesus' overwhelming love draws us, fills us, and marks us with a hunger and thirst that will be satisfied with nothing less than a fresh outpouring of the Holy Spirit—right here, right now. Only a revived church will transform a city, but that can happen faster than you think. Are you ready for an awakening in you, your family, your church, and your city? Here we go!

In the 1950s A.W. Tozer sat reading near a train station where a man was found wandering around, lost and confused. When pressed for information, the man had no idea who he was, where he was, or where he came from. He had lost his identity due to amnesia. The church in America today is suffering a similar malady, as she has no clear sense of identity in Christ or His Word. Yet God has not left His church alone. He is raising up leaders to call the church back to her true, biblical identity. This is not just a corporate church matter, it is also intensely personal, as most individual believers have no clear sense of passion, purpose, or identity. God's spoken purpose over His church is the essential and unifying force to bring the body together and mobilize her to change the world through transforming revival. That is the purpose of this book.

TWEET: @LenRavenhill

If the Lord tarries and there is no revival of pure Christianity, then the next span of years will be the worst history has ever recorded

Many Christians live and die without realizing the perpetual identity that Jesus gives to His people. If we are honest, there are two areas Christians typically feel most guilty about not doing, or not doing well—prayer and evangelism. These are things about which virtually every believer says, "I wish I could pray more," or, "I wish I could evangelize better." Why do we feel this way? Simply because in these two activities is rooted our eternal identity, to be "a house of prayer for all nations" (Mark 11:17). The call to be a house of prayer, and the call to reach all nations, is the heart of what Revival Cry is all about. We feel condemned at the heart of our greatest calling and influence—prayer and outreach. But as the church comes to really embrace who Jesus says we are, then we will be able to perform, through His Spirit, what He is calling us to: prayer and evangelism to change the world. The call to prayer and the call to reach out are intricately joined together, and must never be pursued independently of one another.

It was unlike any other day in the Temple: Jesus fashioned a whip and physically drove out those buying and selling. The story is found in every one of the Gospel accounts, suggesting that its message is of utmost importance to the Holy Spirit and for His church. Personally, the story had never made much sense until I heard Jim Cymbala, the pastor of Brooklyn Tabernacle in New York City, preach a message entitled "My House Shall Be A House of Prayer." He explained that Jesus' anger arose not only because the place dedicated to God had been set aside for making money, but more importantly because the place God had set aside for prayer had been filled with other things. Prayer is simply a relationship or conversation with God. The place for God's people to get to know Him had been replaced. The conversation with God was being interrupted. This provoked unprecedented righteous anger from Jesus. Why? Because the very purpose of the church is rooted in this call to be a house of prayer for all nations. Without prayer, the true identity of the church is lost in confusion. Without prayer, there can be no God-honoring outreach. Without prayer, there will be no community-transforming revival. The Bible and church history attest to these facts.

It would be an interesting day indeed if Jesus showed up physically tomorrow and began driving non-essential things from churches in America. To successfully cleanse the church of the rubble that is hindering prayer, God must begin not with the institution, but with the individuals of which it is comprised. What in our lives is as offensive to Jesus as the buying and selling in the Temple, the place of prayer?

Some of the things that must be driven out are good things, but they are pressing out what is most important: prayer. These non-essentials are stealing the identity of the rank-and-file believer. Most have no idea that Jesus has given them the primary calling and identity of being a house of prayer for all nations. As this is both realized and pursued, the church will again begin to function in the joy—rather than condemnation—of prayer and outreach. After Pentecost, no one had to urge the New Testament church toward prayer and outreach; it was their overflowing identity and purpose. Transforming revival began with prayer in an upper room, and continued in life-giving outreach around the world. Restoring the same rhythm of Spirit-empowered prayer and outreach is foremost on God's heart today.

The dramatic events of Jesus' cleansing of the Temple become very personal to us as we realize that in New Testament thinking we, not a building, are the temple of God. Paul asks a powerful question of the Corinthian church: "Do you not know that you are God's temple and that God's Spirit dwells in you?" (1 Cor. 3:16). He and Jesus, speaking from one source, are addressing the same vitally important topic:

> "Church, do you know that you are the temple of the Holy
> Spirit and called to be a living, breathing house of prayer
> for all nations?"

This should excite you, not scare you, because God's calling upon us to be something always comes with the empowering of the Holy Spirit to fulfill and enjoy it. Set your life goal to become a man or woman of prayer. Jesus gave you this identity! The Spirit gives you the desire and power. But you must pay the price to become what Jesus declares you are and the Spirit empowers you to be.

✔TWEET: @Trey_Kent

God's desire, not just Paul's: I desire then that in every place the men should pray, lifting holy hands without anger or quarreling - 1 Tim 2:8

It was just past midnight in mid-February, 2008. My wife, Mary Anne, and I were prayer-walking our neighborhood in Austin, Texas. Each year our church, Northwest Fellowship, would join other Austin-area churches, led by prayer coordinator Barbara Bucklin of Luke 4:18 Ministry, in covering the forty days leading up to Easter in continual prayer. Mary Anne and I decided to pray by walking the streets near our house. It was a night I will never forget, as I learned firsthand how God can transform someone's destiny and calling in a few short seconds, with just a few words. As we walked, I sensed God say something like this to me, "Wouldn't it be wonderful if thirty-one churches adopted one twenty-four-hour day of prayer each month and My city could be covered in 24/7 prayer?" It was as if fire fell on the altar of my soul. I was overwhelmed by the simple words that had come into my mind with such power. I thought, "That's so simple, someone has to be doing it." But when I got home that night I could hardly sleep because of the excitement of this revelation.

The next day I called Dan Davis, the founding pastor of Hope Chapel

Austin, and the key pastoral leader in the Austin area at the time. I told him of the simple idea of covering the greater Austin area in 24/7 prayer by involving multiple churches. Dan not only gave me his verbal blessing, but soon after came to my office and publicly commissioned me for this task in front of a group of local pastors. The news spread, and since 2009 up to forty churches have adopted a day of prayer each month to cover the greater Austin area in unceasing prayer. The beautiful part of the Unceasing Prayer Initiative, as it has come to be known, is that Baptist, Methodist, Bible, Pentecostal, and charismatic churches, and a wide array of the rest of the body of Christ, join together to pray for unity, in keeping with John 17, and revival, in keeping with 2 Chronicles 7:14.

The key has been for the pastor to catch and promote the vision. Churches may join the group only if the pastor signs up his congregation. As many devoted prayer warriors can attest, it is very difficult to maintain an effective prayer movement in a local church without the support and encouragement of the pastor. We've also had one pro-life organization and several prisons adopt a day of prayer for the city. Asking churches and ministries to adopt one twenty-four-hour day of prayer each month is a reproducible way to encourage citywide prayer, and for the body to begin to function as a house of prayer 24/7. The vision is only getting started in the greater Austin area. We believe God will raise up hundreds of churches who are praying one day a month for unity and revival. We look for this revival cry to continue to spread to more and more churches, resulting in dramatic changes in our cities.

Until that day of revelation in 2008, I was totally in the dark as to the massive worldwide prayer movement that is currently underway. According to the International House of Prayer in Kansas City (IHOP KC), every major city in the United States has a 24/7 house of prayer in it, or is working toward launching one. I learned that in 1999 two major worldwide prayer ministries were launched. Mike Bickle and his IHOP KC began 24/7 prayer and worship in September, which continues today. Meanwhile over in England, Pete Greig and his 24/7 Prayer initiative launched local prayer rooms that have since spread to over one hundred nations, encompassing a wide array of Christian denominations. Greig catalogs his journey in the inspiring book *Red Moon Rising*.

On the Mount of Olives in Jerusalem, the birthplace of the Christian church, the Jerusalem House of Prayer for All Nations has been in prayer 24/7 since 1987. In an article in Charisma magazine entitled "Rise of the Praying Church," The Jerusalem center's founder Tom Hess, captured something of the massive prayer army that is growing around the world:

Asia is leading the world prayer movement today from

Korea, China and Indonesia… as 100 million are praying in what we have termed the "Chopstick Revival."… about 100 million intercessors in Malaysia, Singapore, Philippines, Vietnam, Thailand, Myanmar, India, Bangladesh and Pakistan are preparing the way back to Jerusalem for the King of Glory to come. From New Caledonia, New Zealand, Australia, Indonesia, southern India and the Arabian Peninsula, probably 80 million Christians are praying.

Africa has strong growing prayer movements in Tanzania, Kenya and Ethiopia. In Africa, approximately 75 million intercessors, with many 24/7 prayer watches, join in united intercession. South Africa has one of the stronger prayer movements with more than 100 night and day prayer watches. Prayer movements are growing in Zimbabwe, Congo-Kinshasa and Uganda. John Mulinde, of Uganda, has been leading and encouraging 24/7 prayer with the process of national transformation. In Nigeria, 4 million intercessors in one place prayed all night. A month later, God gave them a Christian president… each month they host all-night prayer meetings attended by more than 1 million people.

Prayer and 24/7 prayer movements are growing all over Brazil. The Christian population has grown from 15 to 30 percent in the last 10 years. Mexico has a growing prayer movement and Colombia is also experiencing revival.

God is strengthening the prayer movements in the Caribbean Island nations. In the U.S., many organizations are encouraging prayer for the nations and world. Prayer movements are growing on college campuses. Prayer movements, 24/7 watches and houses of prayer are growing and multiplying in many U.S denominations.

In Israel, they have been keeping 24/7 prayer going since 1987. At that time, the number of 24/7 houses of prayer in the world was fewer than 25; today there are an estimated 10,000.

Growing prayer movements can be found in Ukraine, as well as in Russia. Elf Ekman, from Sweden, and Finnish Christians are making a significant impact through their prayer movements. Today the prayer movement and houses of prayer are multiplying among the young generation in the Turkish church, which has doubled in the last 10 years, One church in Armenia has grown to 8,000. The indigenous praying church in Iran has grown from 3,000 people at the time of the Iranian Revolution in 1979 to more than 3 million today.[1]

As you can see, the house of prayer is already gathering worldwide in small and large groups, asking God to bring revival to His church and to overflow this passion for Jesus to the lost world. This is revival cry.

You are being invited to step into the identity Jesus has given you as a house of prayer. Doing so is not as difficult as it may seem. As an individual house of prayer you are simply called to pray wherever you go. You become a secret world-changer by spreading the incense of prayer throughout your day, in good times and bad. The Fulton Street Revival that rocked New York City in 1857, resulting in over one million conversions in the United States, began with the prayers of one man—Jeremiah Lanphier.

🐦 TWEET: @ChristineCaine

Sometimes you just have to flat out stand up, pace around the house & have your own Holy Ghost revival prayer meeting. I full on JUST DID!!!

You can also take a major step by joining with one or two other believers and beginning to pray consistently for transforming revival in your family, neighbors, work associates, church, and city. Jesus gives us an amazing and often disregarded promise: "And I say to you, if two of you agree on earth about anything they ask, it will be done for them by my Father in heaven" (Matt. 18:19). Joining with other members of your church and praying for revival and for the churches in your neighborhood is a simple move toward becoming a house of prayer. The prayers of a few college students in Wales lit the fires of a revival that brought historic change to many nations beginning in 1904. The impact of this Welsh Revival is still being studied today.

The most powerful demonstration of a citywide house of prayer is when believers gather together across denominational and local church lines to pray for God to transform their city. This is what happened in Azusa, California in 1906 when a passionate Anglo believer named Frank Bartleman joined William J. Seymour, an African-American preacher, and others in a racially diverse prayer meeting that exploded into a worldwide Pentecostal revival launching countless missionaries and many denominations. Dr. A. T. Pierson once said, "There has never been a spiritual awakening in any country or locality that did not begin in united prayer."[2]

🐦 TWEET: @Trey_Kent

*Over the weekend 47 prayer warriors prayed 24 straight hours for revival in Austin!!
No one left the building for 24 hours!! Amazing!*

In July 2011, I was privileged along with Mary Anne and our daughter Lindsay, to join Pastor Rick Randall and his wife, Faye, Dr. David Smith and his wife, Julie, in meeting Pastor Jim Cymbala in his office at the Brooklyn Tabernacle, prior to the church's regular Tuesday night prayer meeting. Pastor Cymbala said a few powerful sentences about revival that I will never forget. "I believe that before revival takes place in America, two things must occur," he told us. "First, churches must come out from their denominational and internal church focus and work together for Jesus alone. Second, churches must deal with the race issue and become integrated." I believe that the prayer movement in each city or town of America, rather than any one church, is best suited to facilitate congregations working together for Jesus alone, and for bringing all God's beautiful races together to both build relationships and pray together for citywide revival. How pleasing to God is the sound of His one church, without walls or denominations or color or race, crying out together for the transformation of the city! For me, the most impacting, inspiring, and sobering Bible verse speaking about prayer and revival has been 2 Chronicles 7:14:

> "If my people who are called by my name will humble themselves, and pray and seek my face and turn from their wicked ways, then I will hear from heaven and will forgive their sin and heal their land."

Quite simply, this is the reason for this book. The key is found in the first three words: "If My people". The mess we are in as a nation is not because of the lostness of the world—the issue is the lukewarmness of the church! The remedy for the crisis we face in America rests not with the world getting better, but with the church getting revived. We must daily wage war on lukewarmness in our lives. Revival occurs when our passionate love for Jesus is so great that it overflows outside the walls of the church, and begins to bring transformation to the lost community around us. With this definition, true revival cannot be experienced in the safety of our fellowships alone. Revival always begins by transforming those within the church, but then quickly reaches out and changes the lostness of the community outside.

A CITYWIDE STRATEGY

Tim Hawks, the senior pastor of Hill Country Bible Church Northwest, and pioneer of more than twenty churches in Austin, is helping to lead churches in the area to fulfill a citywide vision of "seeing that every man, woman and child has repeated opportunities to see and hear the gospel of Jesus Christ." This God-sent vision is the goal of a revival cry to see a house of prayer in the greater Austin area calling to God night and day for transforming revival. This cry results in the further mobilization of the body to respond practically and passionately, to become the answer to its own prayers. This is a 24/7 work as well. The ultimate goal of revival cry is to see 24/7 prayer (loving God) and 24-7 outreach (loving others) in order to see every man, woman, and child reached with the good news of Jesus Christ.

In 2009, I was listening to Brian Lightsey, the pastor of Life Church in Leander, Texas, pray at the annual National Day of Prayer gathering in Cedar Park, Texas. In all honesty, I was initially put off by his prayer that, in part, went something like this, "Jesus, as we leave today let us walk out and be the answers to the prayers we just prayed." I went home thinking, "That was the dumbest prayer I've ever heard." But later God began convicting and rebuking me, saying that Pastor Brian had prayed His heart: we are to walk in answer to the prayers we pray. That truth, as simple as it is, began to revolutionize my whole thinking on prayer. Revival cry is the marriage of prayer and outreach—crying out to God, and then walking in obedience to fulfill His will on the earth. Hypocrisy occurs when we pray and don't act, or when we act and don't pray. Overflowing joy and transformation happen when we both pray and act.

🐦TWEET: @ScottyWardSmith

Probably one of the best ways to grow spiritually today is to not think about spiritual growth. Just love & serve others

I AM PRAYER

While reading the classic book, *The Hidden Life of Prayer*, I learned for the first time ever that the literal Hebrew translation of the fourth verse in Psalm 109, when David is crying out for mercy in the midst of much opposition and accusation, ends with the phrase "I am prayer."

Think about that. We focus so much of our time and energy on getting out of trials and pains, and we wonder why God delays. We give words of encouragement to help folks get out of ruts and depression. David on the other hand said, "I am being afflicted, but I am prayer!" What a clear and undeniable affirmation for all true believers to find their identity as a house of prayer. We are prayer. We pray day and night, in good times and bad, at work, at home, while driving, in the prayer room, and at the soccer field.

We are prayer!

Jesus is crystal clear as to what is most important to His heart. In Matthew 22:37-40, He says:

> "You shall love the Lord your God with all your heart and with all your soul and with all your mind. This is the great and first commandment. And a second is like it: You shall love your neighbor as yourself. On these two commandments depend all the Law and the Prophets."

This is Jesus' definition of revival. It is what Jesus died and rose again to do in us.

How often do we get focused on other definitions of what revival is or should look like? Revival often involves emotions, but emotionalism is not revival. Revival can include miracles, but miracles are not revival. Revival can bring church growth, but church growth is not revival. Revival by Jesus' definition is falling more and more passionately in love with God—so much so that this love overflows to transform others both inside and outside the church. The challenge for us in the church is to wage war on lukewarmness by falling passionately in love with Jesus, and to daily take this love to the streets of our cities. When revival comes, these mandates will be our consuming zeal, nothing else. Yet, we must not wait for revival to come in some fanciful future, we must pursue God in prayer by meeting the conditions laid out in 2 Chronicles 7:14, and invite more and more believers from our city to join in the revival cry.

The cry for revival is rising from individual and corporate houses of prayer around the world, and even in your own city. Believers are joining together in twos and threes to cry out for revival. Individuals are walking the halls of their workplaces or schools, contending for revival to come "on earth as it is in heaven" (Matt. 6:10). We are called to both pray relentlessly for revival in this generation, and to work unceasingly toward the fulfillment of our prayers.

🐦 TWEET: @OneCry

"The Church is looking for better methods; God is looking for better men." // EM Bounds // men & women of the gospel...will you answer?

In September of 2011, together with several friends, Mary Anne and I had the life-changing opportunity to spend several days at The Dream Center in Los Angeles. You must read Pastor Matthew Barnett's book, *The Church That Never Sleeps*, to understand how much of Jesus' heart is poured out through this special place. We saw it firsthand, and heard testimony after testimony of people who are literally being transformed by the power of Jesus after being hooked on drugs, or involved in prostitution. Immediately upon arriving at The Dream Center on a Wednesday afternoon, we asked if we could join one of the teams on an outreach. Joel Freebairn, one of the leaders, quickly took us a few short miles down the road to Skid Row. We were literally dropped off in what is known as Heroin Alley: drug deals were going on right in front of our eyes, while transvestite prostitutes were soliciting clients. One man shot up with heroin a few feet from me, not caring at all that I was staring in disbelief. This was just one of the regular mission outreaches of The Dream Center. I was surprised by the number of folks I met at the center who had come off Skid Row. They were not only serious followers of Jesus now, but they were pursuing their passion—or "cause within," as Pastor Matthew calls it—to see the world changed for Jesus. This experience in Los Angeles captured what I mean about not waiting around for revival, but going after it daily through radical prayer and outreach.

TWEET: Jason Meyer @WePreachChrist

God never tires of simple, sincere prayers that say "I need You. I need You more than I can say. I need You to be near today." Cry out to Him

SMALL GROUP QUESTIONS

1. What do you think Jesus means when He says, "My house shall be called a house of prayer for all nations" (Mark 11:17)?

2. How do you honestly feel about your prayer life, and your heart for evangelism? Why?

3. Read one of the accounts of Jesus' cleansing of the Temple (Matt. 21:12-17, Mark 11:15-19, Luke 19:45-48, John 2:13-17). If Jesus did that today, what would He be throwing out of our lives, and out of our churches?

4. "Set your life goal to become a man or woman of prayer." Is this a valid life purpose? Is it yours? Why or why not?

5. Did you have any idea of the scope of the worldwide prayer movement? What's going on in your church and city regarding prayer? How can you join in more consistently?

6. Who could you partner with on a weekly basis to pray for personal, family, church, and citywide revival?

7. What does the concept "walk in answer to your prayers" mean to you?

8. How can you begin to see yourself as a living, breathing, walking house of prayer? How will embracing this new identity change the way you live?

REVIVAL CRY ACTION ITEM

Get two others to join you in weekly contending for revival through prayer

CHAPTER 2

YOUR MOST IMPORTANT NAME: MY DELIGHT

"If my people, who are called by my name..."
- 2 Chronicles 7:14

In Luther: The Movie, I was struck by the shocking words Martin Luther used to declare his hatred of God. Such deep-seated anger overflowed because he felt unable to get past his sins, into a merciful relationship with God. He felt the Almighty was "an angry God." That's where many Christians are today—many at least feel He is a "distant God." Most feel they have yet to break through to the kind of Christian life that God purchased for them through Christ.

They know they should love God, but in reality a negative fear, a sense of inadequacy, distance, and uneasiness arises when they think about getting close to Him.

The remedy for Luther came in Romans 1:16-17:

> "For I am not ashamed of the gospel, for it is the power of God for salvation to everyone who believes, to the Jew first and also to the Greek. For in it the righteousness of God is revealed from faith for faith, as it is written, 'The righteous shall live by faith.'"

The freeing revelation is that we are justified, made right with God, by faith alone. Jesus provides the remedy for the shattered relationship between God and man through the shedding of His own blood. The death and resurrection of Jesus gives to all "born again" (John 3:1-18) believers in Christ a new nature that transforms us from existing as enemies of God to thriving as His children. This changes everything! When understood properly, nothing will ever be the same again for the believer who allows this revelation to take root in his heart. How effectively has the blood of Christ been applied to your heart? Is God still your enemy? Do you have the hope of joy in God? The Word of God provides clear and sufficient answers. Let's move ahead to celebrate the restoration of intimate joy purchased for us, both now and for eternity.

🐦 TWEET: @ScottyWardSmith

If we knew how fully God delights in us because of Jesus, our insecurities would melt and our idols would topple

THE FAVOR OF GOD

Since my 2008 encounter with God, where He called me to help establish 24/7 prayer in the greater Austin area, I have been growing in the revelation of God's love. It seems so simple doesn't it? But after pastoring in Austin for twenty years, I see most Christians—including pastors—sadly miss the experience of knowing the delighting, rejoicing, and singing Father of whom the Bible speaks so clearly. There is a deep longing for the overflowing joy in God that Jesus died for us to experience now. Why have we missed or not emphasized these clear teachings of the Bible, that joy in God is available now?

Some are truly ignorant of the basic reason Jesus died—to make us His very own, His beloved (Rev. 5:9). Others know, but have yet to experience this love firsthand. The Bible is clear that God loved you and knew you even before you were born (Eph. 1:4-5). He delighted in creating you out of all the possibilities that could have existed in His infinite mind. He joyfully knit you together in your mother's womb (Ps. 139:13). As Jesus died on the cross, it was to restore relationship with you (1 Pet. 3:18). When He rose from the tomb, it was to give His righteousness and life to you (Rom. 6:4). He arose victorious on your behalf, and brought glory to His Father in saving you—making you His very own, making you a part of His family. Now that's amazing love! This truth of God's relentless love displayed in Christ is foundational to revival cry.

The objective reason that God will forever rejoice in you is because Jesus has shed His blood and Christ is now your righteousness (2 Cor. 5:21). You are now Christ's ransomed child and beloved of God. You are now wrapped in Jesus' righteousness and Father God will always see you that way. Most believers get this in their head, but experiencing the delighting, rejoicing, and singing love of the heavenly Father is another thing. It takes much prayer and battling of old lies with the Word of God to move into experiencing the daily joy of this blood-bought truth. I distinctly remember when my dear friend Mark Juarez, our associate pastor at Northwest Fellowship, called me into his office one day. With tears in his eyes he read a section out of an R.T. Kendall book about the Father's love. That day, as a seasoned pastor who had been saved for over thirty years, Mark had a fresh breakthrough revelation of the Father's love for him. That's what I hope happens to you over and over throughout your Christian life. May you continually explore the depths of infinite love.

God is not mad at you! To some that's a very strange statement. Many believers trudge through life consciously or unconsciously avoiding intimacy with God because of unhealthy fear. The fact that Jesus took all the anger that your sin deserved should be liberating news. The Bible says, "In this is love, not that we have loved God but that He loved us and sent His Son to be the propitiation for our sins" (1 John 4:10). "Propitiation" is an ancient but life-changing word. In basic terms it means "an offering to appease (satisfy) an angry, offended party, " or to suffer wrath to the point that wrath is turned to favor.[3] Do you see that all the anger and wrath that the infinitely perfect God rightfully had against you has been (past tense) paid for fully by Jesus Christ? God surely has loving discipline for us, but no wrath or spiteful anger. He certainly is not pleased with our rebellion or worldliness, but the Father's rebuke is always rooted in loving discipline, not retaliation or retribution. Because of Jesus, you are now forever in God's favor. You can always approach Him with great joy, knowing He will receive you with love every time (Jude 24).

🐦 TWEET: @RandyAlcorn

"Leave the broken, irreversible past in God's hands, and step out into the invincible future with Him." —Oswald Chambers

WATCHMEN ON THE WALL

Revival cry is about seeing this generation of Christians pray and act to see transforming revival begin in us and spread to our family, friends, church, and ultimately to our city and beyond. The foundation for this revival and for the booming worldwide prayer movement is rooted in a delighting, rejoicing, singing God. In Isaiah 62 we find the passage that has inspired the modern-day prayer movement. The key verses are 6 and 7:

> "On your walls, O Jerusalem, I have set watchmen; all the day and all the night they shall never be silent. You who put the Lord in remembrance, take no rest, and give him no rest until He establishes Jerusalem and makes it a praise in the earth."

Here we see God appointing watchmen on the walls to intercede until the city becomes a city of praise. These watchmen are not some special class of Navy Seal Christians. They are simply the "house of prayer" that Jesus identified when He cleansed the Temple in Jerusalem. We, the blood-bought church, are the watchmen on the wall to intercede day and night until Jesus breaks forth to transform our cities into places of 24/7 praise.

A DELIGHTING GOD

The most overlooked part of Isaiah 62 includes the verses just preceding the call for watchmen on the wall. Verses 3-5 are the key to mobilizing a joy-filled, worldwide prayer army that remains on the wall 24/7, and experiences personal and corporate revival:

> "You shall be a crown of beauty in the hand of the Lord, and a royal diadem in the hand of your God. You shall no more be termed Forsaken, and your land shall no more be termed Desolate, but you shall be called My Delight Is in her, and your land Married; for the Lord delights in you, and your land shall be married. For as a young man marries a young woman, so shall your sons marry you, and as the bridegroom rejoices over the bride, so shall your God rejoice over you."

In verse 3, God calls His people "a crown of beauty...a royal diadem." Verse 4 changes the name of God's people from "Forsaken" to "My delight is in her," and from "Desolate" to "Married". The shocking passage continues in verse 5 by revealing that God rejoices over His people "as the bridegroom rejoices over the bride." Please stop and take in what you just read: you are renamed by God as "My Delight!"

A SINGING GOD

Now, let's unfold from God's Word evidence for the singing God. In 2009 I was on a yearly prayer retreat in Mason, Texas with some of the men of my church. God spoke so clearly to me about a passage I had heard, but had not thought about very deeply. He told me that this verse was going to be a life verse for me. It was Zephaniah 3:17:

> "The Lord your God is in your midst, a mighty one who will save; He will rejoice over you with gladness; He will quiet you by His love; He will exult over you with loud singing."

Here we see once again that God is a rejoicing God. But that's not what struck me that day out in the wilderness, praying alone. The last phrase, "He will exult over you with loud singing," hit me so hard. It caused me to ask, "Is this even biblical?" Then I thought, "It must be, because I just read it in the black and white of the Bible!" Having been a Christian for over a quarter of a century at that time, I was dumbfounded to be awestruck with the beautiful and yet unnoticed concept of a singing God.

🐦 **TWEET:** @Trey_Kent

Don't fear/quit:

1. God is present

2. God is mighty to save

3. God is rejoicing over u

4. God's love quiets u

5. God sings over u

A SONG FOR THE WOUNDED

The ramifications of the truth of a singing God must be explored by all God's children. Churches are full of men and women, boy and girls, who are deeply wounded by the angry and negatively shaping words and actions of others. Many believers sit at home, out of fellowship with God's people, because of the painful words and actions of other Christians. The healing beauty of Zephaniah 3:17 is that the song of the joyous God singing over you begins to heal you—literally "save you"—from this pain. It can quiet your bitter thoughts and words, and cause joy to emerge in your heart. It usually doesn't happen overnight, but as you listen more intently to the God singing over you, you will be healed of a broken heart and filled with a joy that triumphs over every past, present, and future pain. Why not join me in claiming Zephaniah 3:17 as a life verse for yourself? Make it a verse you will rehearse and share often. Many wounded saints need to know the truth of a singing God who sings over them, too. As we listen to our singing Father in Heaven, He begins to ground us in the security of His love, and unleashes in us supernatural desire both to spend time alone with Him and to fulfill His will on the earth.

THE REJOICING GOD

Many Christians are familiar with the idea of a God who rejoices, but most only experience this joy minimally or in fleeting ways. The Bible consistently paints God as the most joyous person in the universe and His Son Jesus Christ as the very embodiment of the same joy on earth. Hebrews 1: 9 says:

> "You have loved righteousness and hated wickedness;
> therefore God, your God, has anointed you with the oil of
> gladness beyond your companions."

This passage shows that true joy is built on God's love of His righteousness and on His hatred of evil. A singing, delighting, rejoicing God is not one who winks at sin. He is not a happy grandfather in the sky who allows you to do what you want all the while you are ignoring His will. That's not the God of the Bible. The Bible consistently joins God's joy and

His righteousness together. In fact, none of God's attributes can be played against another. God is a unified being all of whose attributes always work together, never apart. God is always working in holiness as He works in joy. God is working in mercy as He works in justice. The attributes of God are simply ways we look at who God is, but He does not have many parts—He is unified in Himself. This is important to understand, so we don't end up with a theology of "cheap grace" when we embrace a God who sings, rejoices, and delights over us. This Hebrews passage reveals God's Son, Jesus Christ, as the most joyous person ever to be on planet earth. God the Father is the most joyous person ever. So is God the Holy Spirit. The triune God, three persons in one God, is infinitely joyous and loves to share His joy with His people.

Psalm 16:11 reveals truths so powerful that all the body of Christ must claim them for themselves on a moment-by-moment basis:

> "You make known to me the path of life: in Your presence there is fullness of joy; at Your right hand are pleasures forevermore."

Three truths stand out brightly. God will make known to you as His child the path of true life that He wants you to pursue. Primarily this means that pursuing life that is really worth living is found only in Jesus. All else is death. These verses, which are leading us toward infinite joy, begin with the essential element of pursuing "abundant life" in Jesus, not in the world. The world has no joy to give you. It only has death to pass on. "Fullness of joy" is only and always found in the presence of God. Nowhere else can true joy be found. The Bible teaches clearly that God is always present, but we do not always recognize Him (Ps. 139:7-12). Isaiah 6:3 teaches a similar truth, "The whole earth is full of God's glory." This gives hope to every believer, no matter where or in what situation they find themselves. God is already there, and He is ready to be your joy!

Joy is always and only found in His presence. The best way I know to enter into the presence of God is through worship. Psalm 22 paraphrased says, "God inhabits the praises of his people." Translated into Japanese, it reads like this: "God comes down and sits in a big chair in your midst when you praise Him." That's joy!

Only in God is true pleasure found. All other worldly pleasures are counterfeit, and the joy of sin lasts only a moment (Heb. 11:25). Hear the good news and spread the good news that true and lasting joy and pleasure are only found in God.

🐦 TWEET: @TozerAW

"We need to affirm the saints around us because true saints rarely know how great a blessing they are to others." AW Tozer

INFINITE LOVE

1 John 4:19 is the simplest and shortest verse laying out the concept of our infinite God loving or delighting in us, and us loving Him:

> "We love because He first loved us."

The roots of this verse must go down deep into our hearts. The easily overlooked truth of this verse must be mined more deeply. God loved or delighted in us first. His love was not an afterthought, nor simply a result of our obedience. God's delight in us is rooted in the depths of who He is. "God is love" (1 John 4:16). The infinite love of God was enjoyed in eternity past in the relationship between the Father, Son, and Holy Spirit before any created thing existed. God had no need for any other relationship. He was, and is, completely satisfied in Himself. This makes the creation of humans, uniquely made in His image to relate to Him, all the more astounding. God's joy in fellowship within the members of the Trinity was so explosive that He desired to share that love; this is why God created us. God's passion in Himself overflowed with unstoppable zeal to share this infinite love through Jesus Christ with creatures like us. God's love is so glorious that it had to be shared! In John 17:26, Jesus' own words affirm the fact that Father God has brought us into infinite love, the kind that Father God has for Jesus.

> "I made known to them your name and I will continue to
> make it known, that the love with which you have loved
> me may be in them, and I in them."

This has always been the purpose of creation—to glorify Jesus by saving a people to be His very own. A fully delighting God created and saved us to fully delight in us, and to free us to fully delight in Him. Oh, that more believers would experience the delighting love of God!

FUEL FOR NIGHT-AND-DAY PRAYER

The fuel for 24/7 watchmen on the walls crying out for revival day and night is the delighting, rejoicing, and singing God. Until the church embraces this family blessing, we will remain distant, uneasy, and fearful of God. No one wants to get up at 2 a.m., or even 7 a.m. for that matter, to talk to a God they feel is mad at them. You may do that once or twice, but only intense, joy-filled love will drive night-and-day prayer as God lays out clearly in Isaiah 62. In a confirming passage, Isaiah 56:7, God says I will "make them joyful in my house of prayer." God laid out this entire night and day prayer plan so that we could understand that the heartbeat of 24/7 prayer is not duty, but unstoppable delight in a God who is singing, rejoicing, and delighting over His people. We have a loving Father who gives weak and insecure believers like us a new name: "My delight." This new identity changes everything. Now you can approach God freely, humbly, but also boldly as a son or daughter invited in by a joyful Father.

This is my own testimony. After being a Christian for twenty-seven years, and a senior pastor for fifteen of them, I still felt that I did not know how to pray. I was insecure in God even though I loved Him. I wanted to spend time with Him, but in many ways I felt I had disappointed Him and going to prayer with that much regret did not seem very inviting. Many Christians feel guilty about not pursuing their "quiet times" more diligently. Like me, many have bought the lie that God's primary orientation toward them is disappointment or anger. Why would we want to spend time with someone who is mad at us? That's why the truth of Isaiah 62, the fuel of the praying church, must be embraced, meditated on, and experienced by true believers worldwide. We must wield the truth of the Word of God found in Isaiah 62:3-5 to strike a death blow to the root of the lie that God is a moody, displeased Father. This will do more to free you to enjoy God, to intercede for transformation, and to spread the flames of revival than anything else. Together a delighting God and a delighting people bring forth more and more prayer! And as Samuel Chadwick said, "The greatest answer to prayer is more prayer."

TWEET: @MikeBickle

The small prayers of weak and broken people move the heart of God

WHAT IS LOVE?

What does it mean for God to love us? That is a vitally important question that many are answering incorrectly. Some teach that because God loves us He will overlook our sin and rebellion, and allow us to live any way we want, that He will still eternally save us, even if we reject salvation through His Son Jesus. These lies fill the airwaves, and are heard from pulpits around America. But the Bible clearly teaches that Jesus Christ is "the only way to the Father" (John 14:6), and that there is salvation "in no other name" but Jesus (Acts 4:12). Truly we live in the midst of the "great falling away" that Jesus promised would occur in the last days (Matt. 24:10). Pastors and churches are calling evil good, and good evil. The hearts of many are growing cold (Matt. 24:12).

On the other hand, some sincere believers fear the message of a delighting God because they wrongly worry that if they keep focusing on a delighting, singing, and rejoicing God, the result will be selfish "me-centered" Christians. I understand that concern, but the opposite is true. Most believers I know suffer from incredible insecurity when relating to God, to prayer, and to the Word. We must teach believers over and over that God rejoices in them because of Christ, not because of their performance or inherent goodness. It's about Jesus—He gets all the glory. A true work of the Spirit will always make us more God-centered, not self-centered.

In Luke 11, where Jesus teaches His people how to pray, He also gives a life-altering message that both corrects our faulty view of God and teaches us what it means to be loved by Him. In verses 11-13 He says:

> "What father among you, if his son asks for a fish, will instead of a fish give him a serpent; or if he asks for an egg, will give him a scorpion? If you then, who are evil, know how to give good gifts to your children, how much more will the heavenly Father give the Holy Spirit to those who ask Him!"

Do you see that your heavenly Father loves to give good gifts to His children? He is indeed a delighting, rejoicing, and singing Father who loves to bless His children in the way He sees best—not always the way we understand. This passage encourages us to ask and to receive from a Father who is an infinitely better Father than we could ever be, a Father who is overjoyed to give "good gifts" to His kids.

There is more. In fact, this is where it gets really good. This is where we understand what it means for God to love us in the best possible way. The climax of this passage is verse 13, which tells us "how much more will the heavenly Father give the Holy Spirit to those who ask Him!" This is love. This is the overflowing joy of a delighting God. This is the reason He sings. Father God loves to give the Holy Spirit—the third person of the Godhead—to everyone who asks Him. This must be the pinnacle of prayer and the peak of all joy—God delighting to give Himself to His people to be their joy, delight, and song.

God clearly gives us the Holy Spirit so we can delight in Him, not to make it about us. The evidence that a person has truly experienced the delighting, rejoicing and singing God is they become more and more consumed with delighting in, rejoicing in, and singing to their amazing love, God Himself!

GOD-CENTERED LOVE

This shocks many, but to keep us God-centered, He uses affliction to awaken us to His love in new ways. Romans 5:1-5 is a passage I have treasured for years because it speaks of the reasons for our sufferings. It shows that God is building unshakeable character, perseverance, and hope in His people in what some consider a strange way—through hardships. So many think that God's love is only shown in ease, comfort, and speedy answers to prayers. God sees it otherwise. He says true hope and Christlike character is forged in those who suffer well and endure through strong opposition over a long period of time. Our goal as humans is comfort; God's goal is to make us like His Son, Jesus (Rom. 8:29). Because of this glorious goal, affliction is essential. The great joy is that in our sufferings we find and experience the love of God in new heights, depths, widths, and breadths (Eph. 3:18-19). How will you ever know that God can and will meet you in the deepest depths unless you go there to meet Him (Ps. 139:9-11)? Trust me, He's there with you.

Reflect for a moment on Romans 5:3-5:

> "More than that we rejoice in our sufferings, knowing that suffering produces endurance, and endurance produces character, and character produces hope, and hope does not put us to shame, because God's love has been poured into our hearts through the Holy Spirit who has been given us."

Do you see the purpose for your suffering? Do you see that suffering does not mean that you are not loved by God, but that He is setting you up for deeper and more lasting love? Romans 5:5 has become a mainstay of encouragement for me during good times and bad. God is pouring out His love into our hearts by the Holy Spirit. When God wants to love us in the best way possible, He doesn't send a message, a messenger, or physical blessings — He sends us Himself, in the person of the Holy Spirit. God loves us by giving us Himself! God causes us to delight by giving us Himself! God heals us by giving us Himself! God becomes our song as He gives us Himself! Don't miss God in your affliction.

🐦 TWEET: @VOM_USA (Voice of the Martyrs)

"Before prison we heard about God. But in prison we experienced God." ~Chinese house church pastor Sze.

THE ATTRIBUTES OF GOD

For some people this idea of suffering is not good news because they have yet to experience God as a delighting, rejoicing, and singing Father, a

God who is given so they can delight, rejoice, and sing in all circumstances because He is their joy. Because of pain, many doubt God's goodness and look for physical provision alone as the sign of His love. The wounds of a painful relationship with an earthly father, or a church member who deeply hurt us, foster a false concept of God. We must be vigilant to do battle against these lies. As A.W. Tozer says in *The Knowledge of the Holy*:

> "What comes into our minds when we think about God is the most important thing about us…(with this) we might predict with certainty the spiritual future of that man."[4]

Of all the problems facing Americans, none is more important than repairing our dreadfully tainted concept of God. The remedy is not quick or easy, but it is indeed filled with joy unspeakable. In my senior year as an undergraduate student at Oral Roberts University, my systematic theology professor, Dr. Wayne House, gave me a challenge I keep to this day. He urged me, as he did, to read Tozer's *The Knowledge of the Holy* on a yearly basis, to keep my concept of God filled with truth. I would recommend this challenging and life-transforming practice to you. I also recently listened to the audio version of another of Tozer's books, *The Attributes of God*. I cannot recommend both resources more highly. Stick with them as you forge a new and holy concept of God. Find and read regularly other books highlighting the attributes of God, too. This will shape you like nothing else can. As you discover more of who God is in the Bible, or other books, set your reading aside and get on your knees and worship. No issue is more vital for those who want to spread flames of revival far and wide than a biblical and growing view of God.

THE HOLY SPIRIT AND PRAYER

As I began to study prayer seriously I realized that one aspect seems under-studied and too seldom taught in the Christian world — the issue of the Holy Spirit's empowerment. The Bible is crystal clear that we are too weak to pray consistently and joyfully in our own strength. Paul highlights this in Romans 8:26:

> "Likewise the Spirit helps us in our weakness. For we do not know what to pray for as we ought, but the Spirit himself intercedes for us with groaning too deep for words."

This is a very complex passage, but what is clear is that we as believers are too weak to pray well, so God joyfully gives us the Holy Spirit to enable us to pray as He wills. This is earth-shattering news for those who desire to pray. Prayer is not something we must do in our own strength, but something the delighting, rejoicing, and singing God does through us and with us by the Holy Spirit. Prayer is the overflow of the Holy Spirit being poured into our hearts, resulting in cries back to God for His will to be done on earth as it is in heaven. Revival cry is the Holy Spirit crying out through our mouths to bring about the perfect will of God on earth.

This may sound strange, but it's not a teaching foreign to Scripture. In Romans 8 we see another life-giving passage that brings more clarity as to how the Holy Spirit ignites prayer in His people. In verse 15 we see that in the new birth the Holy Spirit puts a new cry within the heart of His people:

> "For you did not receive the spirit of slavery to fall back
> into fear, but you received the Spirit of adoption as sons,
> by whom we cry, 'Abba! Father!'"

Do you see it? We receive "the Spirit of adoption as sons, by whom we cry, 'Abba Father.'" We no longer make our cry to Father God as outsiders, but now we cry as sons and daughters. We are sons and daughters who now pray, not in our own strength, but joyfully led by the Holy Spirit. This is the best news for prayer-weary, devotionally weak Christians who want joy and delight to drive their prayer times. Simply begin joining the cry of the Holy Spirit within you. It's no longer about "right words" being said. It's about a relationship with your Daddy, made possible because you are perfectly righteous in Jesus and because you have been given the Holy Spirit to pray with you. Let the revival cry of the Spirit overflow in joy through you.

A NEW LIFE GOAL

You may be saying, "It's great that God is a singing God, a delighting God, and a rejoicing God, but I don't know how to experience Him." There is a simple answer, but it is infinitely deep. All the joy, delight, and songs of God come through the one treasure of Jesus Christ. All of God's blessings are one—Jesus. Ephesians 1:3 says:

> "Blessed be the God and Father of our Lord Jesus Christ,
> who has blessed us in Christ with every spiritual blessing in
> the heavenly places."

Rejoice: this passage teaches that you have already been blessed with every spiritual blessing because you are now "in Christ." This is a key biblical term expressed consistently in the New Testament. It means that when God saved you He placed you forever "in Christ". This means that you are now in relationship with Christ—"in Him you live and move and have your being" (Acts 17:28)—and can never be separated from Him.

In recent months, I've been meditating on a most inspiring and hope-filled passage. 1 Corinthians 6:17 says,

"But he who is joined to the Lord becomes one spirit with him."

This is overwhelmingly good news. I am now joined to Jesus, and God will never ever again see me apart from His Son. Stop and think about the infinite benefits of this truth. This brings to light the "how" of experiencing the joy, delight, and song of God—it all comes as we set our lives to know, pursue, and love Jesus with all our heart, soul, mind, and strength. Can you lean into this truth? You are now one spirit with Jesus. I don't mean you are God. I mean your heart is in Him so firmly that it's as if you are one — you are one with Him forever. Call on Him from that place of oneness, not from the place of distance. If you've lost that sense of oneness, repent and regain your sense of being "in Christ!" Let 1 John 1:9 lead the way back:

"If we confess our sins, He is faithful and just to forgive us
our sins and to cleanse us from all unrighteousness."

Your new name, son or daughter of God, has given you the ability through the Holy Spirit to enjoy God, to delight in Him as He delights in you, and to hear His healing song currently being sung over you. Now you must set your life in pursuit of knowing Jesus Christ. All the treasures are there. None of them are in work, or in your family, or in money or sex or drugs or sports. All the treasures are in Christ. If you want to know God as joy and delight, and to hear His song, you must realize you have been perfectly fitted with a new name, with the Holy Spirit to empower you, and with incomprehensible oneness in Jesus Christ.

So set the pursuit of Jesus as your life goal. This is what it means to be a man or woman of prayer. All other goals fall short of the clear and simple reason Jesus died for you. He died, first and foremost, so you could "love God with all your heart, soul, mind, and strength" (Matt. 22:37). Secondly, He died so you can share His love with everyone you meet. Set the direction of your heart and affections to pursue the one goal of knowing Jesus and, out of that you will find all the love you need to love others forever. This is where we experience the singing, delighting, and rejoicing God. This is where we become those who passionately sing, delight, and rejoice in God. Let's press on to know Him!

🐦 TWEET: @Trey_Kent

WORSHIP OF GOD THE FATHER, SON & HOLY SPIRIT is the most exhilarating thing a human can experience & it cannot be duplicated by the world!!!

SMALL GROUP QUESTIONS

1. Do you often feel God is angry or distant? Explain.

2. How would you explain to a believer from the Bible that "God is not mad at you?"

3. According to Isaiah 62:6-7, what does it mean to be a "watchman on the wall"? Are you one?

4. How would it change your approach to God if you embraced His new name for you as "My Delight"?

5. Explain Zephaniah 3:17 in your own words.

6. How much of Psalm 16:11 have you experienced? How much more is available? How do you experience more?

7. If we are empty in love, what does 1 John 4:19 reveal?

8. What fuels night-and-day prayer?

9. What is love, or God-centered love, according to the Bible?

10. What do you think Romans 8:26 means?

REVIVAL CRY ACTION ITEM

Take a twenty-four or thirty-six hour spiritual retreat, pressing into the Lord concerning His delight in you and your delight in Him.

CHAPTER 3

YOUR MOST IMPORTANT ATTITUDE: HUMILITY

"If my people, who are called by My name, will humble themselves..."

- 2 Chronicles 7:14

Humility is often seen as dry, joyless, and painful, but the Bible portrays the humble as those who are filled with amazing grace, and joy unspeakable. They have deeply filled hearts. What if I told you the key to revival is humility? And what if I told you that the leaders of the upcoming revival will be unknown, humble, and Christ-exalting folks? In this chapter you will meet a host of characters—some you know and some you don't—who have experienced or are experiencing the explosive growth that results from humility. Their names are John, Peter, David, Tozer, Jose, Mike, Mark, Judas, Marco, and Jesus. Any of them ring a bell?

▼TWEET: @DavidSliker

The primary agenda of the Father in this hour - perhaps more than even love and holiness - is humility, and filling the earth with it.

WHAT'S SO AMAZING ABOUT HUMILITY

The classic devotional writer Andrew Murray calls humility the most important attribute for any Christian to posses because it is the gateway to all other blessings of God. I agree. I just wish it were easier to live humbly! Right now, God has untold blessings that He's ready to pour out on you. The only hindrance is (fill in your own blank). For most of us the answer is pride. God must take us down in humility so He can lift us up in blessing. Why? So it never becomes about the blessing, the glory, the gift, or the goal—it always remains about God!

JOHN: THE GREATEST

John the Baptist is the greatest example of humility. Why? Because Jesus said so! Jesus called John the Baptist the greatest person born of a woman from the time of Adam to the time of Christ. Now, that's a compliment! Can you imagine Jesus using you to define humility to your generation?

Why was John so great? I believe John's own words show what Jesus called greatness:

"He (Jesus) must increase, but I must decrease" (John 3:30).

The essence of John's greatness was his humility. Is it really true that to be great is to be humble? I don't think you'll read that in Success magazine. I don't think "the Baptist guy named John" would ever have made the cover of Jerusalem Success Stories. Humility is making much of Jesus, and in the process forgetting about yourself. That's not a popular notion in most businesses, or even churches. John lived for one purpose — to make much of Jesus. This is the sole reason he's our greatest example of humility.

The context of John 3:30 reveals that all of John's followers were going to Jesus. In other words, John's ministry was crumbling, his business failing, and his future growth projections were shattered. John understood that greatness is not found in making more money, obtaining more friends, becoming better looking, landing a prestigious job, or securing a hefty stock portfolio. Do you see how anti-American humility really is? We want to see flat-out prosperity, growth, and popularity. But according to the only book that really matters, you can succeed in all these areas and be a total failure in God's eyes. Success in God's Word is always rooted in humility—making much of Jesus in all things. The coming revival will be led by humble men and women.

✔TWEET: @OneCry

Humility is nothing but the disappearance of self in the vision that God is all. // Andrew Murray

A NEW FOCUS

To be humble can be both the easiest thing in the world and the most impossible. As I set aside time to write this chapter, God began filling my morning with more and more interruptions—people in need, pastors requesting information. One after another, the distractions came at me full force. It was all good stuff, but it became intensely frustrating. That's when I realized the distractions were not sent by the enemy to ruin my day, but sent by God to bring me to a place of humility. These distractions were a gift, to cause me to choose humility. Honestly, it's not always easy to see that God has a bigger agenda in all circumstances. In one way, humility is easy because we are given daily circumstances that can cause us to let Jesus increase and force decrease in our stature. Yet, it's impossible to humble ourselves unless God is center-stage of our focus in any given circumstance. Then, it's not about us anymore. This is humility.

PETER: A FIRST-CENTURY AMERICAN?

Most Christians I know are thrilled the Apostle Peter is in the Bible. Seriously, we love him because we identify with his brash, extroverted nature that so parallels the American persona. Peter promised much and delivered little — until Acts 2! That's when everything changed. Peter understands better than most what it means to say, "I'll be faithful to the end," and then to fail miserably in Jesus' very presence (Luke 24:54-62).

I wonder if that's why Jesus restored Peter and raised him up to such a high level in the New Testament church. Peter not only preached the opening message which launched the early church, but also wrote two challenging and encouraging books in the Bible. Prideful Pete was transformed into Humble Pete.

In Peter's first book, we find what for me has been the most helpful passage regarding humility:

> "Humble yourselves therefore, under the mighty hand of God so that at the proper time He may exalt you" (1 Pet. 5:6).

Peter knew that without a clear and awe-filled view of God and His glory we can never be humble. We will only be victims of our own self-sufficiency. Humility is not putting ourselves down. That can actually be a sneaky way of pridefully making ourselves the center of attention once again. Humility is not saying you are a worm. Humility is forgetting about yourself as you exalt Christ and serve others. That's what Peter learned—that it wasn't about him. We humble ourselves under God's mighty hand: a moment-by-moment battle. It is our joy to say, "Jesus, this situation is not about my comfort or notoriety or respect—it's about You and Your glory." Humility begins and ends as we make much of Jesus in all situations.

🐦 **TWEET:** @KVMMinistries (Kris Vallotton)

I am hidden in Christ. It's the greatest disappearing act of all times!

DAVID: A STRIKING REVELATION

David was the least likely in his family to be king. When the prophet Samuel showed up to anoint the new king, David was out watching sheep and no one even considered him to be a candidate for the royal position. David quickly became famous after defeating Goliath, and being named King of Israel. That's when it got rough for him. His humble seeking of God was replaced by arrogance and self-promotion, which eventually led to the grave sins of adultery and murder. The lessons of humility needed to be learned all over again. Psalm 51 is one of David's most well-known prayers, and a compelling portrayal of his journey back to humility. It's a must-read for all. In the Psalms David reveals what made him great in God's eyes.

Psalm 119, the longest chapter in the Bible, is most often attributed to David. Please take time to read this incredible passage. The theme of almost every verse is the Word of God. David is filled with deep passion for the Word, and deep disdain for those who don't keep it. The Psalm overflows with amazing, God-spoken truth, with no obvious hint of humility, until the astounding final verse. In verse 176, we read words that seem to be totally out of sync with the message of the previous verses:

> "I have gone astray like a lost sheep; seek your servant, for
> I do not forget your commandments."

This verse jolts us out of complacency and faithfully drives home the true benefit of meditating on God's Word. Digging into the Word brought David to one overwhelming conclusion: "I have gone astray like a lost sheep!" That is the fruit of the Word of God born in the life of a man or woman who is humbly being trained by it.

Paul warns believers, "Knowledge puffs up, but love builds up" (1 Cor. 8:1). The danger of amassing more knowledge for knowledge's sake is pride. When we are seeing God's glory and greatness, and being deeply convicted by the Word, we are brought to a place of humility and love. Thankfully David's failures produced in him humility, and therefore God memorialized him as a "man after God's own heart." That's the goal of every humble believer.

TWEET: Pray Always! @erotao

If we only spent more of our time in looking at Him we should soon forget ourselves.- Martyn Lloyd-Jones

TOZER: HUMBLING QUESTIONS

How do you know if your Bible knowledge is leading you to pride or humility? Take this quick five-question test:

- Am I educated beyond my level of obedience?
- When I read the Bible do I first find things others need to change?
- Do I make excuses as to why I can't obey the Bible?
- Is my reading of the Bible more about me than about Jesus?
- Am I often frustrated because circumstances don't work out for me?

If you answered yes more than no, then I believe you need to join me in repenting of pride and humbling yourself under God's mighty hand, that He may lift you up in due season.

You've probably already realized I love to read Tozer. I call him my mentor from afar. He died in 1963, the year I was born. Yet Tozer inspires me immensely to grow in pursuing, understanding, and desiring the majesty of God. One of the most convicting and humbling of his writings includes seven questions of self-judgment. Why not get out a journal and honestly answer them before God?

1. What do I want most?

2. What do I think about most?

3. How do I spend money?

4. What do I do with leisure time?

5. Whose is the company I enjoy most?

6. Whom and what do I admire?

7. What do I laugh at?[5]

The most helpful part for me of these convicting questions is found in Tozer's explanation: "Where we go when we are free to go where we will is a near infallible index of character." Do you see what Tozer is saying? When we are free to do what we want to do, and free to hang out with whomever we choose, our choices are the truest tests of our character. This is so important. Let me restate it very simply: the truest test of your character is what you do, and with whom you do it. Humility is forged as we seek God when no one's watching, and when we choose to build relationships that both honor Christ and lead others to know and honor Christ. All else is mere talk. Tozer forged humility the same way we must, by being awestruck by God's greatness over and over again.

🐦 TWEET: Pray Always! @erotao

Nothing sets a person so much out of the devil's reach as humility. Jonathan Edwards

JOSE: INSIDE-OUT HUMILITY

The most important part of humility is that which no one sees except God. Becoming a humble person is not a public undertaking. Weakness, dependence, and integrity are forged as believers lay their lives before God in prayer. Jesus teaches us, "When you pray go into your room alone"

(Matt. 6:6). He is telling us how to avoid pride and how to build humility at the same time. Humility comes through prayer, and prayer is ultimately seeking God. If we refuse to meet with God in secret, we will never know public or private humility. Humility is forged in the secret place with God. As we allow God's loving holiness to transform us from within, we are made humble.

I love the story of Jose Joseph. I first met him in 1997. Born in India and raised in a lower caste, Jose didn't own a single pair of shoes until he was twenty-two. But God had an amazing future for him as he pursued God in the secret place. God provided miraculously to send Jose to Youth With A Mission (YWAM) in Lindale, Texas. Jose's stories of God's miraculous intervention while he was waiting faithfully at the airport, with no known provision, sound like something out of the book of Acts. Yet they occurred in the life of a humble, modern-day disciple from India. Jose is now the director of the YWAM base near Mumbai, India. How did he break out of the chains of poverty and hopelessness? The simple and unexpected answer is: humility.

Practical humility is submitting oneself to be taught by the Holy Spirit through the Word. That's what Jose has done. Humility is not coming up with your own thoughts, ideas, or insights. It's exchanging your thoughts and your ways for His thoughts and His ways (Isa. 55:8-9). Throngs of believers refuse to be taught by the Word, and so they remain infants, pride-filled babies more concerned with their opinions than with God's truth. God-given humility is forged in prayer and Bible study in the secret place. Long hours with God bring the teachable into a place of transformation within. Jose's long and often lonely hours with God have prepared him to be a new kind of leader—a humble leader that God can use to change the world.

The key to transformation is being changed from the inside out. The popular Hillsong chorus proclaims:

My heart, my soul, Lord I give you control

Consume me from the inside out Lord

Let justice and praise become my embrace

To love You from the inside out

Most believers are focused on ordering their outer world, but God brings revival from the inside out. Believers must get radical about receiving God's Word and Spirit on the inside, over and over throughout the day. This is what humility looks like: believers refuse to think their own thoughts and refuse to focus first on outward success. This is the foundation for the building of humility. It is built inside. The tests often come from outside, but the true work of humility comes as we submit to God. If we say we want to be humble, but do not as a lifestyle seek God in the secret place, we deceive ourselves. Seek God in secret through long hours of prayer and the Word. This is the garden of humility that will produce abundant grace upon the earth.

✈TWEET: @ChristineCaine

Humility is not thinking less of yourself, it is thinking of yourself less!

MIKE: VOLUNTARY WEAKNESS

Mike Bickle, the founder and director of the International House of Prayer in Kansas City (IHOP-KC), uses a term that makes very practical the concept of humility. It is "voluntary weakness." Mike teaches that through regular fasting and the regular sacrificial giving of time and money, we voluntarily make ourselves weak so Jesus can change us and become our strength. Fasting is a difficult discipline, but one that Jesus assumes believers will adopt as a lifestyle when He says, "When you fast..." (Matt. 6:16). Fasting helps us grow spiritually by making us weak physically. In like manner, we become weaker financially as we give away money and weaker in time as we give it away. But at the same time we put ourselves in the perfect position for God to move in His strength. In fact, Isaiah 58 links true fasting, helping the poor, and revival together. The question must be asked, "Are you satisfied with your strength and your resources, or do you want God's resources?" To get God's resources, we must regularly, as a lifestyle, let go of ours. Giving up our resources and receiving God's resources is what true revival is all about.

Mike refers to the community he leads at IHOP-KC as a group of weak and broken people who are fascinated with Jesus. That sounds like humility to me. As IHOP-KC pursues 24/7 prayer and worship, they are daily overwhelmed with human weakness. Can you imagine being a part of a community that has been pursuing night-and-day worship nonstop for fourteen years? That would make you humble.

MARK: ROOTS OF HUMILITY

A powerfully moving example of humility is one I've encountered firsthand as I pastor Northwest Fellowship. I met Mark Juarez, then the pastor of Living Hope Foursquare Church in Cedar Park, in 1997. He has since become our associate pastor at Northwest Fellowship, and one of my closest friends. The amazing gift for me has been Mark's teachability, humility, and servanthood. He is about twenty years my senior, and could have easily said, "I know more than you. You are the age of my son, and I won't submit to you." But he adopted a completely different attitude. For more than ten years Mark has worked closely with me, serving humbly in every task set before him. Whether voluntarily picking up trash, serving the poor, counseling those in need, moving to another country to serve others, or doing anything imaginable to fulfill the Great Commission, Mark's life is a shining example of humility.

What are the roots of this humility in his life? Having watched firsthand, I know that Mark spends hours at the beginning of each day praying, reading the Word, and worshiping God with his wife, Pat. There are no short cuts. A humble servant of others must first become a humble servant of God when no one is watching. I respect Mark so much as a pastor and friend, but the quality I most admire in his life is his humble submission to Jesus. This allows Mark to work with those younger and less experienced with a servant's attitude because he has, as a lifestyle, submitted to God. What a living example of a humble life.

TWEET: @JustinBuzzard

"How much larger your life would be if your self could become smaller in it." -G.K. Chesterton

JUDAS: AN ENEMY OF HUMILITY

Can you believe that one of Jesus' chosen disciples, Judas, epitomized the absolute opposite of humility? What are the biggest enemies of humility: pride, fear, immaturity, self? Judas had them all! Pride was the root of Judas' problems. He loved himself. Pride raises itself up against God and longs to rule. Pride is the enemy of all enemies, and must be dealt with by a death blow from the cross. You cannot clean up pride. The Bible warns that "pride goes before a fall" (Prov. 16:18). God refuses to share His glory with another (Isa. 42:8). As the cross does its work, the believer submits to God in secret and this allows God's grace to overflow in public.

Fear is a cousin of pride and lurks around to coerce believers into hiding from God and from relationships with others. Normally fear is rooted in hurt. Jesus gives a foolproof remedy to heal fear:

"Perfect loves casts out fear" (1 John 4:18)

As God brings believers face to face with their worst fear, He sends His love to heal the wound of fear, and to free them to walk in joyful humility. Much of the body of Christ in America is in a state of immaturity. We tolerate the half-hearted pursuit of God and we obey only that which is pleasing to us. Many parent their children toward happiness instead of maturity and end up raising spoiled-rotten kids. God has a greater goal than our happiness. His goal is that we look like Jesus (Rom. 8:29). Since this goal is foremost in God's mind, He will never Father us toward immaturity. The Holy Spirit is given to lead us to maturity in Christ. This is the hallmark of a humble life.

Day in and day out, the biggest visible enemy to humility is self. Self is the practical outworking of pride. Our old self rises up to take center stage in our life and dethrone God from His rightful place. Self is an insidious monster that slickly and selfishly refuses to obey God, and has its own form of logic to maintain control of the heart. Self, like all other enemies of God, has one remedy—death by crucifixion. The Bible says to "consider yourself dead to sin but alive to Christ" (Rom. 6:11). God works this daily death through orchestrating circumstances to crush our pride and drive us back to God. Hebrews 12:6 says that "the Lord disciplines the one he loves, and chastises every son whom he receives." This is not a wrath-filled discipline, but a measured, loving, and caring crucifixion—yes, you can call crucifixion loving and caring—of our old life and old ways.

MARCO: SIMPLE OBEDIENCE

At a lunch with several pastors gathered to plan a citywide day of prayer event, Pastor Marco Noriega offered a powerful picture that speaks clearly of the need to obey to receive God's full blessing. He noted how when Jesus told the disciples to wait for the coming Holy Spirit there were probably five hundred there to pray. But as the days went on, many got discouraged and left. By day ten only a hundred and twenty remained. "What if those one hundred and twenty had quit on day nine?" Pastor Marco asked. "On day ten the Holy Spirit was poured out, and that has changed the entire world!"

We must press on to receive God's promised blessing. The humble person perseveres by the grace of God. Are you on the verge of an unknown blessing? Don't quit!

In the same vein, what if Joshua and the children of Israel had circled Jericho obediently for six days, but quit before the seventh day when they had to walk around the city seven times and shout to receive the victory? Or, what if Naaman had dipped in the river only six times, refusing to dip one more time? He would have missed his healing. Humility launches believers into bold obedience in response to His Word. Humble people refuse to take matters into their own hands, or subject the Word of God to human logic. Humble believers obey and meet God in new and amazing ways because of their obedience.

What is Jesus calling you to do? Have you obeyed? Are you teachable? The Bible says that when Jesus walked the earth, He only did what He saw the Father doing, said only what He heard the Father saying, and did nothing of Himself. That is true humility lived out by the God-man, Jesus Christ. How different would our lives be if we lived totally listening to the voice of God? Prayer would be much different if, like Moses, we saw our relationship with Almighty God as a friendship (Exod. 33). Look at it like this: your best friend knows all things, rules the universe, and lives inside you. He is ready 24/7 to give you the wisdom you need to follow Him!

Jesus told His disciples that servants are different from friends. Servants do not know their master's business. Jesus made this astonishing proclamation in John 15:15:

> "No longer do I call you servants, for the servant does not know what his master is doing; but I have called you friends, for all that I have heard from my Father I have made known to you."

Doesn't it make sense that if Jesus calls us friends who know what He is doing, then an important component of humility is simply listening to His direction and obeying it to the end?

We must not look to Jesus simply as our model, but we must acknowledge His desire to lead us into the life of humble obedience that He led on the earth. Can we be better equipped? Christ in us, the hope of glory, is constantly present to lead, encourage, and strengthen. We must learn the joy of submitting to His voice and pursue the adventure of obeying Him radically day in and day out. The Christian life will indeed become that which God meant, the greatest adventure ever!

🐦 TWEET: @CSLewisDaily

We must get over wanting to be needed-this is the hardest of all temptations to resist

JESUS: THE HUMILITY OF GOD

The most surprising truth about humility is that the most humble person in the universe is also the Creator of the universe. In Philippians 2:3-8, we find the clearest definition of humility:

> "Do nothing from selfish ambition or conceit, but in humility count others more significant than yourselves. Let each of you look not only to his own interests, but also to the interests of others. Have this mind among yourselves, which is yours in Christ Jesus, who, though he was in the form of God, did not count equality with God a thing to

be grasped, but emptied himself, by taking the form of a servant, being born in the likeness of men. And being found in human form, he humbled himself by becoming obedient to the point of death, even death on a cross."

We are taught to live humbly on all occasions, and that this means to live not for our own interests but also for the good of others. Humility must be a mindset, an attitude that puts self aside in the exaltation of another, God Almighty. Jesus, as we've seen, lived in perfect and humble dependence upon His Father, and for the glory of God and the good of others. Humility takes "self focus" out of the equation and causes us to live as stewards of God in all moments. Ultimately, humility is obedience. Jesus is the perfectly humble God-man. He obeyed even to the point of death, death on a cross.

I've heard it said that pride is thinking we deserve better than Jesus got. He was raised in a poor family—more than likely his father died when he was young. He never went more than two hundred and fifty miles from home, He suffered extensively in life, and was forsaken by all in His young death at age thirty-three. He had no home, and had to catch a fish with a coin inside to pay His taxes. Do you see how amazingly blessed we are? We deserve hell. We don't deserve any of the blessings we've received—physically, emotionally, financially, relationally, spiritually. We don't deserve the Father's love. We didn't earn the favor of Jesus. We couldn't have been good enough for God to call us "the temple of His Spirit.". We are blessed in order to make much of Jesus.

TWEET: @DavidSliker

Regardless of how you think today went, rest assured: you received far, far more than you deserved from the God who loves you well.

SMALL GROUP QUESTIONS

Define humility in your own words.

1. JOHN: Why did Jesus call John the Baptist the greatest man born of a woman?

2. PETER: What does 1 Peter 5:6 teach us about humility? How have you experienced this truth?

3. DAVID: Consuming the Word of God can lead to either pride or humility. Why?

4. TOZER: Which of his seven questions of self-judgment is the most convicting for you? Why?

5. JOSE: What does the statement that "humility is birthed from the inside out" mean?

6. MIKE: Jesus teaches us to live lives of voluntary weakness in fasting, serving, and giving. Why do you think Jesus asks us to give our lives away? How can this result in a more humble life?

7. MARK: Who is a key example of Christlike humility to you?

8. JUDAS: What is the greatest obstacle to you living a life of humility?

9. MARCO: What are you currently facing that could result in a mighty harvest of blessing if you persevere?

10. JESUS: What does living the crucified life mean? How can hardship, problems, and humbling circumstances actually be blessings in disguise?

REVIVAL CRY ACTION ITEM

Fast and pray for revival one day a week.

CHAPTER 4

YOUR MOST IMPORTANT ACTIVITY: PRAYER

"If my people, who are called by My name, will humble themselves, and pray..."
- 2 Chronicles 7:14

Jesus tells a shocking story in Luke 18:9-14. Two very different men went to the Temple to pray. One was a highly esteemed Pharisee—especially in his own eyes — while the other was a disdained (and usually dishonest) tax collector. The Pharisee's prayer was perfectly eloquent:

> "God, I thank you that I am not like other men: extortioners, the unjust, adulterers, or even like this tax collector. I fast twice a week; I give tithes of all I get." The tax collector's prayer was raw, honest, and full of repentance as he beat his chest: "God, be merciful to me, a sinner."

Jesus follows up this story with a revolutionary analysis of the men's prayers: "I tell you, this man (the tax collector) went down to his house justified, rather than the other. For everyone who exalts himself will be humbled, but the one who humbles himself will be exalted" (Luke 18:14). This passage gives great hope to people like us who don't feel we really know how to pray "correctly." The parable must have been highly contradictory to the prevalent thought patterns of the day. I wonder today if, like our biblical predecessors, we've exalted the prayers of men and women whom God rejects and have rejected the prayers that God accepts. The devil has greatly hindered the prayer lives of many believers by shaming us for our meager prayer lives. Yet the key to prayer, according to this parable, is not flowery words, special techniques, or creative models. The key to prayer is honesty, humility, and repentance. In fact, Jesus promises that the humble pray-er will be exalted. I believe by "exalted" Jesus means we will be brought to enjoy God's presence more and more. That's the highest end of prayer!

🐦 TWEET: @GrahamCookeBBH

"Prayer is finding out what the Father wants, then standing in Christ before Him and asking Him to do it by the power of the Holy Spirit."

As I have become increasingly involved in the global prayer movement in the past few years, I have gained much by reading, worshiping, and praying both in person and online with believers worldwide. Yet one thing surprises me. I hear little talk about or focused effort on praying the way Jesus taught us to pray. It seems rather crazy to me to neglect the Lord's Prayer when the biggest question I face in prayer is, "How do I pray correctly?" Jesus answers that question by clearly and concisely laying out His pattern for prayer. Jesus told us in this parable that those who humble themselves will be exalted. Isn't it a humble thing to follow the clear orders of Jesus Christ when praying? Let's explore the way Jesus says to pray.

Think of all the books and all the words that have been written on prayer. Many volumes exist, in both the ancient and modern church. Jesus, on the other hand, teaches us to pray in just fifty-two words:

"Our Father in heaven,

Hallowed be Your name,

Your kingdom come,

Your will be done, on earth as it is in heaven.

Give us this day our daily bread,

and forgive us our debts, as we also have forgiven our debtors.

And lead us not into temptation, but deliver us from evil"

(Matt. 6:9-13)

Jesus introduces this short, transforming prayer with these words: "Pray then like this!" Now we are getting somewhere! We see that a humble-hearted prayer life following Jesus' prayer guide is most pleasing to Him and most beneficial for us personally, for the church worldwide, and for reaching the lost.

The seven themes in the Lord's Prayer are closest to God's heart for us! I like to see them as seven circles of revival, or circles of encounter. More than anything else, Jesus wants us to experience God in these truths in prayer. When these seven areas of prayer are followed—not legalistically, but from the heart—they will produce more spiritual transformation than any other prayer that could be offered.

JESUS' PRAYER GUIDE: Seven Circles of Revival

1.   Experience God as Your Father.

2.   Treasure God and His name as holy.

3.   Intercede for God's reign to come and His will to be done.

4.   Ask for today's needs to be met.

5.   Receive and give total forgiveness.

6.   Request protection from temptation.

7.   Cry out for deliverance from evil.

CIRCLE ONE: EXPERIENCING GOD AS YOUR HEAVENLY FATHER

God's first priority is for us to experience Him as our Father. Prayer is not only a place of dialogue with God, but it's also the reality of our growing intimacy with Him. Nothing is more important for a healthy and thriving prayer life and a restored emotional life. In Psalm 23:3 David makes this joyful statement: "He restores my soul." This is at the heart of the first cry of the Lord's Prayer: "Our Father." Fathers give children a sense of security, identity, vision, and direction. We have an epidemically fatherless generation—at least in a human sense. As the years pass, I see the blessing of aging, especially in ministry. Getting older gives me the privilege of being a father figure to the up and coming generations. This is often the most effective place in ministry. Likewise, God's first agenda is that all His people experience Him as Father. This is not a foreign concept, even to those who have enjoyed little or no fathering in their lives, since God has now adopted us:

> "For you did not receive the spirit of slavery to fall back into fear, but you have received the Spirit of adoption as sons, by whom we cry, 'Abba Father!'" (Rom. 8:15)

The verification of our adoption is that we have been given the Holy Spirit inside us, and by the Spirit's enabling we naturally cry out "Abba Father," or Daddy! Inherent to your new birth in Christ is your healed relationship with your heavenly Father. Remember, Jesus says, "Our Father in heaven!" He's not talking about your broken and less-than-perfect earthly dad. Jesus is calling us to a place of safety, healing, security, love, and relationship as we relate to His perfect Dad and now our perfect Dad. Prayer becomes the setting for Father God's love to heal our broken hearts and restore our fractured minds. All this occurs in the place of prayer. Jesus' first desire is our knowing, enjoying, and receiving from God as Heavenly Father.

🐦 TWEET: @64Fellowship

"Prayer is the way the life of God is nourished." Oswald Chambers

How does experiencing God as Father actually occur in the place of prayer? The Holy Spirit within leads us to relate to God as Father and to receive the benefits of adoption as sons and daughters. "The Spirit himself bears witness with our spirit that we are children of God," says Romans 8:16. The whole atmosphere of prayer is set as we receive love from our heavenly Father and give love back to Him. Establishing your relationship with Father God is the vitally important first circle of revival or encounter. Many experience prayer as talking to the sky, or feeling that their prayers do not rise above the ceiling. The Bible has good news: "You are God's temple" (1 Cor. 3:16). Your prayers are immediately heard by God who lives inside you! Prayer is an actual conversation, a relationship, with a real Person who loves you more than you will ever know! Jump into the first circle of prayer—Experience and enjoy your heavenly Father!

FOUR TIPS FOR EXPERIENCING YOUR HEAVENLY FATHER

1. Begin by worshiping Father God and enjoying His presence. He's real!

2. Exalt one aspect of His Fatherhood that blesses you!

3. Ask the Holy Spirit to reveal where you need to be Fathered today!

4. Ask Father God to heal any obviously hurt areas of your heart

---

CIRCLE TWO: TREASURING GOD AND HIS NAME AS HOLY

"Hallowed be Your name" is actually a prayer asking that we would, as a community of followers of Christ, treasure God's name as holy. The importance and need of this reality has never been more pertinent. As Tozer eloquently teaches, "No religion has ever risen above its conception of God." This means that if our God is small, our life will be small. If our God is weak, our prayers will be weaker still. If our God is tainted, our prayers will soon cease to be. But, if our God is big, our prayers will be full of faith. If our God is powerful, our prayers will access the unmatched resources of God. If God is holy, our prayers will seek to treasure God's unique glory.

What does it mean to treasure God as holy? The word "holy" can mean pure, untainted, or perfect. R.C Sproul, in his wonderful book *The Holiness of God*, describes "holy" as being set apart or "other," meaning that God is unlike anyone or anything else. Wayne Grudem says in *Systematic Theology*, "God exists in a fundamentally different order of being."[6] He is infinite, unmatched, and unequaled in every way. He is infinitely, without degree, above all creatures. Tozer says that "God is as high above the highest archangel as He is above a caterpillar." God, in His glory, exists in infinite perfection which can never change, grow, decrease or diminish.

Jesus invites us to treasure and experience God in His holiness. Only in this amazing journey toward the unfiltered nature of God can we become holy as He is holy. Through condemnation, shame and doubt, the enemy tries to keep us from walking toward and experiencing God's transforming holiness. In my younger years as a believer, I bought the lie that God's holiness was to be avoided. Scores of believers worldwide do the same. The enemy has taken one of the rarest and most transforming experiences of prayer away from scared, shamed, and fearful believers. This must end!

Jesus paid a great price, His very life, to ensure that we can proceed boldly and with full assurance into the most holy place:

> "Let us then with confidence draw near to the throne of grace, that we may receive mercy and find grace to help in time of need" (Heb. 4:16)

> "Therefore, brothers, since we have confidence to enter the holy places by the blood of Jesus" (Heb. 10:19)

> "For our sake He made Him to be sin who knew no sin, that in Him we might become the righteousness of God" (2 Cor. 5:21)

> "Now to Him who is able to keep you from stumbling and to present you blameless before the presence of His glory with great joy" (Jude 24)

All believers have been dressed in the righteousness of Christ and are made ready for the awe-inspiring journey of seeing and enjoying the jaw-dropping "otherness" of God's holiness. Many believers remain infants because they have yet to take their rightful place as sons and daughters of the King. They have not realized that they can walk into the holy of holies of God's presence and be transformed:

> "And we all, with unveiled face, beholding the glory of the Lord, are being transformed into the same image from one degree of glory to another. For this comes from the Lord who is Spirit" (2 Cor. 3:18)

Transformation comes from beholding God in His holiness. No gazing = no glory experienced. How many believers have been cheated out of the blood-bought privilege Jesus earned for us to regularly see and experience God's holiness? No more, child of God! Jesus urges us as a community and individual believers to wrap ourselves in His righteousness, and walk toward God's holiness in prayer. Transformation results each and every time.

How do we actually treasure God's holiness? Can we really enter this circle of holiness and encounter God? Yes, but we must see honoring and experiencing God's holiness as our highest good. As we begin to think rightly and pray boldly, we will desire God and His holiness above all things. In this pursuit, we will mine the scriptures, growing more and more in the experiential knowledge of God's holiness. Prayer is the place where we call on the Holy Spirit to lead us in both treasuring and experiencing God's holiness. Apart from the Spirit, we can do nothing. Experiencing and treasuring God's holiness becomes a reality—"Not by might, not by power, but by My Spirit," says the Lord (Zech. 4:6). God invites us into this circle of holiness to be transformed by His unmatched glory. This is the place where revival within occurs. Heed God's invitation to treasure His holiness above all else!

🐦 **TWEET:** @Trey_Kent

Prayer is the essence of Christianity...it's how we have a relationship with Christ & get marching orders to change the world!

CIRCLE THREE: INTERCEDE FOR GOD'S REIGN TO COME AND WILL TO BE DONE

In circle one, we experience the Father. Circle two invites us to encounter God's holiness, and now circle three is the place we ask for God's kingdom—His reign, rule, and will—to be done on earth as it is in heaven. This is the intercessory circle of Jesus' prayer guide. The Bible highlights the vital importance of intercession in the following passages:

> "And I sought for a man among them who should build up the wall and stand in the breach before me for the land,

that I should not destroy it, but I found none" (Ezek. 22:30)

"But Moses implored the Lord his God and said, 'O Lord...Turn from your burning anger and relent from this disaster against your people...And the LORD relented from the disaster that he had spoken of bringing on His people" (Exod. 32:12-14)

"You must also help us by prayer, so that many will give thanks on our behalf for the blessings granted us through the prayers of many" (2 Cor. 1:11)

"For I know that through the prayers and the help of the Spirit of Jesus Christ this will turn out for my deliverance" (Phil. 1:19)

"Your kingdom come" and "Your will be done" are parallel prayers. Praying for God's kingdom and will is equal to praying for God's Word to be done. Praying in line with the Word of God is essential to God-honoring prayer. Deuteronomy 29:29 says, "The secret things belong to the Lord our God, but the things that are revealed belong to us and to our children forever, that we may do all the words of this law." When we pray "Your will be done" we are actively asking, according to God's revealed will, for His Word to be fulfilled on earth as it is in heaven. The Word reigns supremely in heaven; our prayer in this section is that the Word would reign right here, right now.

Nothing is more vital, important, or exciting than for the will of God to be done and for God's kingdom to come in a particular area or situation. As we pray for God's kingdom reign to come and will to be done, we cry back to God His Word and promises related to situations we are facing. This is the reason that knowing, loving, memorizing, and rehearsing the Word is vital to praying as God directs. A very practical way to pray for God's reign and God's will to be done is to ask for God's kingdom to come first in your life, then in your family, neighbors, church, city, nation, and world. In each area, we ask several key questions.

1. Ask God, "Where do I or others need your kingdom rule most today?" Listen.

2. What promises or Scriptures can you pray back to God? Pray.

3. Ask God where your heart or life is out of line with His word. Repent.

4. Ask God how to pray His Word over your family, neighbors, church, city, nation, and world. Obey.

Praying for God's kingdom to come and for His will to be done is the heart of revival cry. Jesus' ministry revealed the power of God's kingdom in a unique way. Pentecost, in Acts 2, reveals the coming of the kingdom in dramatic and transformative power. As the body of Christ today, we cry out for God to send His Spirit to bring transforming revival to individuals, couples, families, churches, neighborhoods, city, states, and nations. We each must begin with this prayer: "Jesus, send transforming revival to me, my family, my church, and my city today!" We must settle for nothing less: Jesus died to bring revival and we must contend for it today!

🐦TWEET: @RickWarren

6 Way God answers prayer: Yes; No; Not yet, You be the answer, Trust Me, and Are you kidding me?

CIRCLE FOUR: ASK FOR TODAY'S NEEDS TO BE MET

"Give us this day our daily bread" is the cry of a humble, dependent child of God upon his or her Father in Heaven. The simple desire to ask our Heavenly Father in faith is rooted in our trust of His goodness. In teaching us to ask, seek, and knock, Jesus reveals the unwavering kindness of His Father to "give good things to those who ask Him" (Matt. 7:11). He says "Or which one of you, if his son asks him for bread, will give him a stone? Or if he asks for a fish, will give him a serpent? If you then, who are evil, know how to give good gifts to our children, how much more will your Father who is in heaven give good things to those who ask him!" (Matt. 7:9-11).

Asking God for daily bread has caused me to see God's intricate goodness in phenomenal ways. In 2003, God moved our church from a secure and stable building in a comfortably middle-class neighborhood to a 37,500-square-foot warehouse that needed hundreds of thousands of dollars of work. This mission field and all its needs were more of a challenge than our three-hundred-and-fifty-member, middle-class church had resources to handle. As the years passed, the church slowly began to fall behind on our rent payments. Even though over the almost ten-year period we had paid over a million dollars in rent, we still found ourselves five months—eighty-five thousand dollars—behind on our monthly commitment. To say that I and the leaders of our church were stressed and burdened is an understatement. We prayed many, many times for God to provide our "daily bread" so we could pay our owners.

We found that God moves in mysterious ways.

In November 2012, Mary Anne and I decided that we would take full ownership of the church debt and sell our house to begin paying it off. I approached our landlords with a desire to make this debt right, a humble and timid heart, and the reinforcement of prayer and fasting from our church body. In a display of grace we could have never anticipated, the benevolent owners of our space informed me that they were forgiving all the debt we owed them—and that they wanted to renew a lease with us! Never in a million years could we have expected God to answer our prayers for daily provision in the time and way He chose. God answers our prayers in the most perfect way and best timing to most clearly reveal His glory. We must never think that daily bread is first and foremost about us. Even our needs are meant to reveal the goodness and wisdom of a perfectly loving heavenly Father. As you begin to ask God to meet daily needs, remember that He is able to do "far more than you can ask or think according to His power that is at work in you" (Eph. 3:20-21) Ask some simple questions to help you pray for daily bread:

- What are my biggest needs spiritually, relationally, emotionally, and financially?

- Do my prayers reveal how big I know my heavenly Father is?

Having pastored Northwest Fellowship for twenty years, one thing I have learned for sure is that needs never go away. You can't wait until all your needs are met to have joy in God. Joy in God is not based on everything being perfect on earth. Our joy is based on the fact that God is perfect, and His presence is always available to bring us joy. He is our joy! "In your presence is fullness of joy and at your right hand pleasures forever more," declares Psalm 16:11. Never allow the delay of your needs being met, or the fact that they are not met according to your timetable, to keep you from enjoying a daily passion for Jesus. He is delaying only to set you up for a greater miracle in His perfect timing.

🐦 TWEET: @OneCry

Unforgiveness & revival cannot exist together in the same space. To choose revival is to choose forgiveness.

CIRCLE FIVE: RECEIVE AND GIVE TOTAL FORGIVENESS

"Forgive us our debts, as we also have forgiven our debtors." According to author and teacher R.T. Kendall, revival would break out in America if we simply obeyed this one verse. Why? Most of us walk around with walls between us and God, and between us and others. These walls steal our passion for God and stop revival within us. The simple act of repenting, receiving forgiveness from God, and giving forgiveness to others begins to launch us toward personal revival. Remember, revival is when the first commandment to love God overflows outward into the second commandment to love others so powerfully that it begins to bring change in society.

I recently read a powerful tweet from pastor and author Ray Ortlund that reveals a major need in America: "God is not a talent scout, He's a Savior. Need saving?" Until we admit we need saving, or that we have offended a holy God, we will never stop, repent of (turn away from) sin, and confess our rebellion against God. This is the reason most Americans remain unsaved, and most churchgoers are unchanged. Change happens through repentance. Revival always occurs as men, women, boys, and girls experience deep conviction, turn from sin, and pursue loving Christ with passionate, Holy Spirit-empowered zeal.

Many see conviction of sin as shameful and condemning. Sin is indeed full of shame, but conviction of sin by the Holy Spirit is actually the most love-filled gift God gives to us. He loves us so much that He invites us to leave our death—and sin is death—and turn to Him for life. Conviction is not God's rejection; rather, it is His acceptance of us! Conviction is God's invitation to a new life. David reveals deep trust in the character of God by praying as we should:

> "Search me, O God and know my heart! Try me and know
> my thoughts! And see if there is any grievous way in me,
> and lead me in the way everlasting" (Ps. 139:23-24)

This deep trust and love of God is why, even though he committed murder and adultery, David is described by God as "a man after my own heart" (Acts 13:22). Those who will experience God-sent personal revival will trust Him to expose the sin and rebellion rooted deeply in their lives. They will celebrate the surgery, even though it will be painful and heart-wrenching. What follows will be well worth the pain. Acts 3:19-20 urges:

> "Repent therefore, and turn again, that our sins may be
> blotted out, that times of refreshing may come from the
> presence of the Lord, and that He may send the Christ
> appointed for you, Jesus."

Refreshing not only occurs as we repent and receive forgiveness from our heavenly Father, it also occurs as we forgive those who have sinned against us. We often harbor the sin of unforgiveness against those who have sinned against us. It is a crazy and delusional way to punish others. As the classic illustration portrays, we drink poison thinking it will hurt the one with whom we are angry. The result is a wounded, weak, self-focused, and dead heart. But God has a sufficient remedy—"forgiving each other; as the

Lord has forgiven you, so you also must forgive" (Col. 3:13). Are you forfeiting personal revival, deep joy in God, and influence on the earth because you are retaining a sin or hurt for which Jesus has already paid the price? Let go of the sin, offense, or hurt and allow God to bring times of refreshing in and through you today.

The application is simply this, ask:

- Jesus, what sin is keeping me from you right now?

- Jesus, whom do I need to forgive now as you have forgiven me?

🐦 TWEET: @Trey_Kent

Prayer is the one thing God says to do without ceasing.

CIRCLE SIX: REQUEST PROTECTION FROM TEMPTATION

"And lead us not into temptation" is the wisest prayer against evil, for it sets the goal of winning over temptation before it occurs. This request also acknowledges that God is the only one who is able to "keep us from stumbling and to set up before His glorious throne with great joy" (Jude 23-24). God reigns over every molecule in the universe—including all evil. "All things exist by Him and for Him—including all thrones, powers, rulers and authorities," says Colossians 1:16. The famous Dutch politician and theologian Abraham Kuyper wrote, "There is not a square inch in the whole domain of our human existence over which Christ, who is Sovereign over all, does not cry: 'Mine!'"[7]

The cry for protection is a daily request from the heart of weak, broken, and dependent people like us. Paul shows us where our power is: "I boast all the more about my weakness...Christ's power is made perfect in my weakness" (2 Cor. 12:9). Yes, we are forgiven, righteous, and made-new creatures, but we remain one hundred percent dependent, often weak, unsure, and totally looking to Christ as our protection, power, joy, and significance, and to be our all and all, moment by moment. Having been saved for over thirty years now, I can testify to the fact that our strength in the Lord is revealed through daily dying to self while being broken by circumstances. In this brokenness, God does His deepest work to make us like His Son (Rom. 8:29, James 1).

Many say temptation is inevitable, but the Bible teaches that although temptation is common to all (1 Cor. 10:13), we can ask God to remove it from us before it occurs. Practically speaking, God can give you the strength ahead of time to avoid tempting situations. The best and most effective weapon against temptation and evil is truth and righteousness in the innermost being. In his heart-wrenching confession after adultery and murder, David claims "You desire truth in the inmost being" (Ps.51:6). This truth, hidden in our hearts by storing the Word within (Ps. 119:9-11), is the sword of the Spirit that brings a deathblow to sin, temptation, and evil. For centuries, spiritual giants have taught us clearly that the victory over temptation and sin is won in the secret place, long before the confrontation occurs. As James 1:14 warns, temptation rises from within, so the best offensive strategy against it is a renewed mind and a clean heart.

Practical steps in praying this passage include asking God to:

- Protect your mind, body, and spirit against temptation.

- Give you a hunger for His Word, and for prayer.

- Fill you with His Spirit today.

CIRCLE SEVEN: CRY OUT FOR DELIVERANCE FROM EVIL

"But deliver us from evil" is the final cry of the Lord's Prayer. This is a bold request asking God to free us from Satan's power and from the lures of the lust of the eyes, the lust of the flesh, and the pride of life (1 John 2:15-17). Ephesians 6:12 reminds us, "For we do not wrestle against flesh and blood, but against rulers, against the authorities, against the cosmic powers over this present darkness, against the spiritual forces of evil in the heavenly places." Our real war is not against humans, but against Satan and his demons. May the Lord deliver us from wrongfully focusing on the people who are confronting us or our agendas. Other humans may be against us in some way, but they are not our enemies. And if they behave as enemies, Jesus gives the following admonition:

> "But I say to you who hear, Love your enemies, do good
> to those who hate you, bless those who curse you, pray for
> those who abuse you" (Luke 6:27-28)

Some of the most prevailing evils we need to be delivered from are fear, self-focus, paranoia, skepticism, hatred of others, and unforgiveness.

In our cry for deliverance from evil, we must put on the full armor of God. Ephesians 6:14-18 instructs:

> "Stand therefore, having fastened on the belt of truth, and having put on the breastplate of righteousness, and as shoes for your feet, having put on the readiness given by the gospel of peace. In all circumstances take up the shield of faith, with which you can extinguish all the flaming darts of the evil one; and take the helmet of salvation, and the sword of the Spirit which is the word of God,

praying at all times in the Spirit, with all prayer and supplication."

To fight the good fight of faith, we must daily put on the armor of God which includes truth, Jesus' righteousness, sharing the gospel, faith, assurance of our salvation, the Word of God, and prayer. To effectively live in victory over evil, believers must learn to leverage these godly tools.

The most insidious battle and the most difficult war with evil is not fought on the outside or from difficult circumstances alone—it is won or lost within. Jesus affirms this by teaching, "For out of the heart come evil thoughts, murder, adultery, sexual immorality, theft, false witness, slander" (Matt. 15:19). To be "delivered from evil," we must allow the Holy Spirit to deal with the secret battles with evil within by confession of sin, repentance, being washed with the blood of Jesus, being filled with the Holy Spirit, and by renewing our minds with the Word of God. 1 John 2:15-16 warns, "Do not love the world or the things in the world. If anyone loves the world, the love of the Father is not in him. For all that is in the world—the desires of the flesh and the desires of the eyes and pride in possessions—is not from the Father but is from the world." This raises the bar in dealing with evil, and confronts practical American cultural issues like over-eating, enjoying inappropriate movies and books, indulging in the love of material things, and embracing countless other idols. These tolerated evils come from a love for the world and can only be rooted out by "considering yourself dead to sin, but alive to Christ" (Rom. 6:11). As believers, we must refuse to give ourselves a pass because we feel our sin is okay. It's not: it is killing us and our families. Join me in asking the Holy Spirit to conduct a deep and difficult inventory of the things we've tolerated that are sin.

The good news is that when we pray "deliver us from evil," we can be sure that the One we are calling out to both understands our battle and has soundly defeated the world, the flesh, and the devil. As you pray for deliverance from evil, rehearse the following verses:

"Greater is He who is in me than he who is in the world" (1 John 4:4)

"He disarmed the rulers and authorities and put them to open shame, but triumphing over them in him" (Col. 2:15)

"But thanks be to God, who in Christ always leads us in triumphal procession and through us spreads the fragrance of the knowledge of him everywhere" (2 Cor. 2:14)

"If anyone is in Christ, he is a new creation. The old is gone, behold all things become new" (2 Cor. 5:17)

"So you must also consider yourselves dead to sin and

alive to God in Christ" (Rom. 6:11)

A PRAYERFUL PURSUIT

Nothing is more telling in revealing the true state of the heart than prayer. One great old said saint said, "As a man prays, so is he." In other words, our lives in Christ will never be greater than our prayer lives. When we as Jesus' people on earth pray the way He taught us to pray, we will begin to see more and more revival fire breaking out in our lives, and in the lives of those around us. This fire fuels a deep and growing passionate love for Jesus and an overflowing compassionate love for others. Prayer deals with our inner life so we can live outwardly through Jesus' power, to accomplish His will on the earth. To neglect the inner life is to set yourself up for daily failure. To pursue God through praying the Lord's prayer is the best preparation for daily walking in the Spirit and daily walking in Jesus' will and purpose.

Set yourself a simple goal this year—to become a man or woman of prayer. All other goals pale in comparison with this pursuit.

TWEET: @Trey_Kent

The heart of true prayer says:

Our Father

Your Name

Your Kingdom

Your Will

Give us

Forgive us

Lead us

Deliver us

SMALL GROUP QUESTIONS

Why is prayer seen as such a daunting task, rather than a delightful relationship with an incredible God?

1. CIRCLE ONE: Why do you think it's vitally important that we have a real and ongoing experiential relationship with our Heavenly Father?

2. CIRCLE TWO: Read Isaiah 6:1-8, then discuss how seeing God's holiness can be both ruining and healing at the same time.

3. CIRCLE THREE: What do you learn as you read over the scriptures about prayer in this section? Do you think your prayers for others really make a difference? Why or why not?

4. CIRCLE FOUR: What is your testimony about God providing your daily bread?

5. CIRCLE FIVE: What in your life are you still battling that you've already asked God to forgive? What situation are you still working to forgive? No need to name names!

6. CIRCLE SIX: In what specific area do you need victory over temptation right now?

7. CIRCLE SEVEN: Claim one of the passages noted below as your victory over evil and addictions. Declare it in front of the small group. For example: "Romans 6:11 says I am dead to alcohol and alive to Christ. The power of addiction is broken in me by the cross!"

   "Greater is He who is in me than he who is in the world" (1 John 4:4)

   "He disarmed the rulers and authorities and put them to open shame, but triumphing over them in him" (Col. 2:15)

   "But thanks be to God, who in Christ always leads us in triumphal procession and through us spreads the fragrance of the knowledge of him everywhere" (2 Cor. 2:14)

"If anyone is in Christ, he is a new creation. The old is gone, behold all things become new" (2 Cor. 5:17)

"So you must also consider yourselves dead to sin and alive to God in Christ" (Rom. 6:11)

REVIVAL CRY ACTION ITEM

Focus on one of the seven circles of prayer each day.

CHAPTER 5

YOUR MOST IMPORTANT FOCUS: GOD

"If my people, who are called by My name, will humble themselves, and pray and seek my face..."
- 2 Chronicles 7:14

In his book *Not A Fan*, Kyle Idleman asks, "If following Jesus cost you everything, would it still be worth it?"[8] It's an amazing question that reveals so much about us. But before you answer casually yes or no, let's unpack it a little. If following Jesus cost you your job, would it still be worth it? If following Jesus cost you your house, would it be worth it? If following Jesus cost you your health, would it be worth it? If following Jesus cost you your family, would it be worth it? If following Jesus cost you all your money, would it be worth it? If following Jesus cost you all your time, would following Jesus still be worth it? If following Jesus cost you your favorite hobby, would it be worth it? If following Jesus cost you your very life, would it be worth it? Think deeply about each scenario.

TWEET: A W Tozer @TozerAW

"The glory of God always comes at the sacrifice of self." AW Tozer (The Crucified Life)

Now, if following Jesus cost you everything, would it still be worth it?

_____Yes or **_____No**

Here's the hard truth: we answer that question every day by the way we choose to think, pray, live, love, and act. The roots of each individual's response are found in one key answer that drives all others: who is God, and what is He like? Is He worth giving up everything for? To reset our hearts and minds toward the goal of giving up everything for Jesus, we must answer some very basic questions that men and women have been asking since the beginning of time:

- Who is God?

- Who is man?

- What is mankind's purpose?

- What happens when you die?

According to the Bible, God is the Infinite Creator of the universe. He is completely holy, loving, personal, and transcendent; He took on human nature in Jesus Christ to rescue sinners who receive Him. You'll find these truths in Genesis 1:1, 1 Peter, 1 John, John 17:3, Philippians 2, and John 1:12. Furthermore, men and women, the unique apex of creation, are made in God's very image (Gen. 1:26) and for His own glory (Isa. 43:7). Man's purpose was destroyed with Adam's sin, whereby all humans inherit a sinful, rebellious heart toward God (Gen. 3, Ps. 50:15, Eph. 2:1-3, Rom. 3). Only in Jesus Christ can men, women, boys, and girls find their true purpose, which is to know Jesus Christ and make Him known to others (John 17:3, Matt. 28:18-20). Death is not an end, but a beginning. For believers, death ushers us into eternal joy and purpose (Phil. 1:21, Rev. 21-22). But the unbelievers' death ushers them into eternal damnation where there will be no relief for eternity (Matt. 25:46, Mark 9:4, 2 Thess. 1:9).

How a man answers the question, "What is my purpose?" will determine for what or whom he lives and dies. If God is indeed real, then He is the only object worthy of sacrifice. The greatest evidence of God's reality is that God the Son became a part of this creation in order to lead lost humanity to a relationship with Father God. This is a historical fact, as is His mighty resurrection from the dead. The resurrection validates everything Jesus said and did. The clearest and most undeniable proof of God and His nature is found in the life, death, and resurrection of Jesus Christ (Acts 2:22-24). If you want to understand the character of God, look at Jesus. God is exactly like Jesus because Jesus is God in the flesh. Jesus conquered sin and death to become our eternal purpose, now. He is our purpose!

Most Christians I know would agree wholeheartedly with all this. Yet when life is boiled down to affections, schedules, and balance sheets, pursuing God rarely gets first place. Could it be that most of us preachers have missed the mark in our sermons, leading people to believe that doing good and living right is the goal of life? Could it be that most parents have yet to teach and model for their children the unending purpose of all of creation? No more common words are heard in the Christian church than, "The purpose of humans is to know God." However, there is no more clear rejection of this truth than can be seen in the day-to-day lives of most American believers.

The Bible could not be more clear as to the simple purpose that transcends all else. Acts 17:26-27 says (emphasis added):

"And He made from one man every nation of mankind to

live on all the face of the earth, having determined allotted periods and the boundaries of their dwelling place, that they should seek God, in the hope that they might feel their way toward Him and find Him."

Think about this: your one purpose is to seek to know God personally. Really? Aren't we to put equal time into being good parents, spouses, employees, change-agents, and so on? Listen to these shocking words by Jesus in Matthew 7:21-23:

"Not everyone who says to me, 'Lord, Lord,' will enter the kingdom of heaven, but the one who does the will of my Father who is in heaven. On that day many will say to me, 'Lord, Lord, did we not prophesy in your name, and cast out demons in your name, and do many mighty works in your name?' And then will I declare to them, 'I never knew you; depart from me, you workers of lawlessness.'"

Take note of the following five facts from this passage, from Jesus' own mouth:

1. Words alone will not get you into heaven (vs. 21)

2. Spiritual gifts, power, and good works alone are not in and of themselves "doing the will of God," and won't get you into heaven (vs. 22)

3. Jesus' not knowing us is the ultimate reason anyone is ever refused entrance into heaven (vs. 21, 23)

4. Not being known by Jesus equals not doing the will of God (vs. 21, 23)

5. When Jesus doesn't know us, all our works are evil (vs. 23)

A simple summary: having Jesus know us means doing the will of God, and is the one and only reason people get into heaven for eternity. When Jesus "knows us" we know Him and pursue Him as the goal of life.

TWEET: A W Tozer @TozerAW

"We are not diplomats but prophets, and our message is not a compromise but an ultimatum." AW Tozer

Could the reason for an anemic church be that we are not pursuing the one purpose Jesus says is essential? Could the only remedy for a lukewarm church that has lost her first love be seeking God as the sole priority? I believe so!

Why don't we seek God? If we are honest, it's because we don't know how. We don't think it's worth the time and energy. We are pursuing things we can see, touch, and feel. Finally, we don't seek Him because the God we have embraced is so small that He's boring.

Five Remedies to Reclaim Our Purpose:

1. Recapture the awe-inspiring, mesmerizing, and utterly intoxicating beauty of God in the Word.

2. Ask God for a fresh outpouring of the Holy Spirit to escort you into the deep things of God.

3. Develop your heart and mind to be able to spend long hours with God alone.

4. Sacrifice time, money, hobbies, and relationships in order to know Him.

5. Set your heart to pursue the goal of God for decades and decades.

RECAPTURE

Jesus' assessment of the church of Ephesus, in Revelation 2, is a fitting one for the church today:

"But I have this against you, that you have abandoned your first love" (vs. 4)

Jesus affectionately defines the relationship between God and His children as first love—not first obligation, duty, or discipline. As you read the Bible, read it to see, worship, and experience the glorious grandeur of God. Read the Bible to fall in love. As you read, slowly meditate. Stop and experience the God you just read about. Seeing God in the Word must result in worship in your daily life. Worship Him in real time—now! This pursuit will begin to revive your first love. You will move from seeing the Bible as words on a page to experiencing it as a pathway to develop the most dynamic relationship with the most attractive person in the universe.

TWEET: @Trey_Kent

"W/ the veil removed by the rending of Jesus' flesh, w/ nothing on God's side to prevent us from entering, why do we tarry without?" AW Tozer

Jesus tells the church of Ephesus to "Remember therefore from where you have fallen; repent and do the works you did at first" (Rev. 2:5). Remember the passion you had at first, how you spent hours pursuing Jesus and feeling zeal in your heart for Him? Has Jesus ever been your first love? If not, begin today. Cry out to God, "If I have nothing else I will not rest until You become my first love!" If Jesus has been your first love and your love has grown cold, remember the former passion and repent by turning back to Him now. Repentance is not a negative thing; repentance is the most amazing gift God ever gives humans. Repentance begins with conviction by the Holy Spirit. Conviction of sin is not condemnation, it is not a negative. It is an invitation to a new life. Embrace Revelation 3:19-20:

> "Those whom I love, I reprove and discipline, so be zealous
> and repent. Behold, I stand at the door and knock. If anyone
> hears my voice and opens the door, I will come in to him
> and eat with him, and he with me."

Conviction is an invitation to deep fellowship: make sure you open the door! This challenge was written by Jesus to the church. He is showing us that His own people have closed the door to deep fellowship with Him. You must open that door to deeper intimacy with Jesus.

We are exhorted to remember, to repent, and to do the works we did at first. At first, when you were a new believer, you probably sought God with joy. But somehow, in the busyness of growing up as a Christian, all the "church" duties crowded out your pure and simple calling to seek God. Today, remember, repent, return, and engage in intentional seeking of God. Even now, set this book aside and spend time remembering, repenting, returning to, and seeking God for no other reason than the fact that He is so jaw-droppingly amazing!

✈TWEET: Wigglesworth Quotes @S_Wigglesworth1

The life that is in us is a thousand times bigger than we are outside.

A FRESH OUTPOURING

Nothing is more needed today than a fresh outpouring of the Holy Spirit—a new Pentecost. Nothing will remedy our lukewarm ways like fresh fire from heaven (Matt. 3:11). The Bible has good news for those seeking revival from a fresh outpouring of the Spirit. In fact, the most unclaimed and seldom experienced promise from God's Word is found in Luke 11:13:

> "If you then, who are evil, know how to give good gifts to
> your children, how much more will the Heavenly Father give
> the Holy Spirit to those who ask Him!"

Jesus is inviting us to experience a fresh, reviving outpouring of the Holy Spirit. Ask!

- Do you want revival in your heart? Ask!

- Do you need revival in your family? Ask!

- Do you long to see your church burning with holy fire? Ask!

- Do you long to see your neighborhood and city transformed? Ask!

Ask for a fresh outpouring of the Holy Spirit to come upon the church. Claim Luke 11:13. Hold up God's promise to Him and humbly tell Him you will keep asking, seeking, and knocking until you, your family, your church, your neighborhood, and your city experience a modern-day move of the Holy Spirit. This honors God. John Wesley said, "Give me 100 men who love nothing but God and hate nothing but sin and I will change the world." Be one of those men and women who are contending for a fresh move of God. Why shouldn't it begin with you? And why not right now? Wesley also said, "Get on fire for the Lord and people will come from miles to watch you burn." The Holy Spirit is the one who sets the believer on fire, so ask!

Luke 11:13 is our rallying cry in this day. We are the people who stand on the promises of God and won't relent until the knowledge of God covers the earth like water the sea (Hab. 2:14). Jesus taught us to pray "Your kingdom come and your will be done on earth as it is in heaven." That is revival! In the fifty-two transforming words of the Lord's Prayer, Jesus said to "pray like this." He taught us to pray daily for revival on earth as it is in heaven. This passage is our amazing invitation to ask for revival. Jesus taught us to ask daily because He promises to answer with a modern-day Pentecost. Don't let this make you nervous; it's simply God's promised response in Luke 11:13 to pour out the Holy Spirit upon those who ask. Revival Cry's purpose is to help mobilize a modern-day prayer army that is contending night and day for a new Pentecost. Nothing less will do. You are one of those modern-day contenders for revival. Begin now, and settle for nothing less.

LONG HOURS

Recently our church sent a twenty-one-year-old college student to be an intern with the International House of Prayer in Kansas City. I was shocked when he told me that as part of the internship training, he spent close to forty hours a week in the prayer room. Could you ever imagine spending so much time doing nothing but seeking God's face? "Hold on," I hear you say, "I can barely spend fifteen minutes in a quiet time." Believe me, I know the struggle. Most of us never push through and outlast the distractions that rob us of spending long hours alone with God. But without that time before the Lord, we will never know Him the way He deserves, or the way we deeply desire.

Let me give you a challenge. This very week, why not find a church prayer room or a house of prayer in your city and commit to spending two hours a week there for the next year? If you do this, you will spend a hundred and four hours alone with God. I'd encourage you to spend those two hours in one setting. Force yourself to stay there for two hours whether you are bored, distracted, or feeling unproductive. Take your Bible, a journal, and some favorite worship music, and go for it. Allow the Holy Spirit to uniquely orchestrate your time with Him each and every time you enter the prayer room. Don't go with a formula; go for an encounter. God will meet you! If you don't have a prayer room near you, create one. Joe and Mona Elliott, our dear friends and associates at church, created a prayer room in their house for family and friends to meet with God. Be creative, find or make a place of prayer—one set aside for God and you alone.

🐦 TWEET: @Trey_Kent

Spiritual disciplines are fuel to love HIM more, not a means to earn HIS love--we already have that. Disciplines allow us to experience love

A good friend of mine was working for a company that was connected to a local house of prayer when I first met him. He wasn't always a prayer warrior. In fact, when he went to work for this Christian company, all employees were required to spend regular time in its on-site prayer room. The catch was that my friend wasn't even saved, yet. According to his own testimony, he was addicted to smoking weed. But as he continued to go to the prayer room, out of duty, God met him in a powerful, saving, and delivering way. He was transformed from an unsaved addict to a powerful and dedicated prayer warrior, simply by being before God in the prayer room. I believe the same future awaits you, whether you are a believer or an unbeliever. *Red Moon Rising* tells the story of a new generation's inspiring testimony of 24/7 prayer. Prayer spread across the world from England through Pete Greig and a bunch of tattooed and pierced teenagers who were horrible at praying. The secret: they just did it! God met them in their prayer room because they showed up. Through their weakness, God birthed a worldwide prayer movement that continues to grow to this day. Who knows what awaits you in the prayer room?

Praying is like riding a bike, or tying a tie. You can't learn by reading about it, or watching a video. You must experience it firsthand. You must see God for yourself. He must become your God, your friend, your first love. This love relationship will not happen without long hours in His presence and in His Word. There are no shortcuts. If you are willing to take this challenge, please e-mail me so I can begin praying for you. And I invite you to e-mail me the results, a before-and-after testimony, as you spend two hours each week with the one who loves you most. You can write to me at trey@northwestfellowship.com to let me know how Jesus is changing your world two hours at a time! Going to a prayer room or a house of prayer is essential; you need to get out of your normal environment and into one that is set aside exclusively for fellowship with God. I see the results every week personally as I spend time in our church's prayer room, and hear testimonies from folks who have committed two hours weekly to being there.

Just as a marathoner begins training with a few steps and a few miles that quickly turn into dozens of miles and then 26.2, so the prayer warrior arises. Two hours a week is just a beginning. This obviously does not replace your daily time with the Lord Jesus; it is only a challenge to stretch your prayer life. After one year you could be ready for an internship at a house of prayer, or to increase your time to six, eight, or even ten hours a week before God in the prayer room. Why? To get to know the King of Glory, the One who made you, and the One who saved you. To bring you face to face with both the reason the universe exists and your eternal purpose of fellowshipping with Him. Begin this week: He is so excited to meet with you!

TWEET: @PaulWasher

I have never regretted one sacrifice in Jesus' Name. My only regret is how much I have held back and how little I have lived for Him!

SACRIFICE

King David, a man after God's own heart, said, "I will not take for the Lord…burnt offerings that cost me nothing" (1 Chron. 21:24). To become men and women who "seek His face" we must refuse to give God leftovers. Tozer warns, "God gets leftovers…We tend to give Him that which we don't need instead of giving Him that which we need." Yet, for this new generation of prayer warriors, God must get our best. True worship must be 24/7. God deserves nothing less. Paul clearly teaches this "sacrificial and total worship" in Romans 12:1:

> "I appeal to you therefore, brothers, by the mercies of God, to present your bodies as a living sacrifice, holy and acceptable to God, which is your spiritual worship."

For "the generation of those who seek Him, who seek the face of the God of Jacob" (Ps. 24:6), nothing but the sacrifice of our very lives— including the best of our time, money, energy, skill, and relationships—will do.

Let's get very practical. Kyle Idleman begins *Not A Fan* by recounting a time when he was sitting in the empty sanctuary of the church he pastors, trying to plan a message that would appeal to those who only came to church at Christmas and Easter—something that would draw them in and change their lives. When he opened his Bible to John 6, God began to open his eyes to the fact that Jesus did not entice people with miracles and free meals. In fact, Kyle saw that Jesus' message was so offensive that it actually reduced the crowds. He recounted how Jesus "cut off" those who followed Him only to get their stomachs filled. Jesus confronted them with the call to feast on Him as the nourishment for life. It offended many. In many of our churches today we are trying to entice people into loving Jesus instead of calling them to forsake all gladly for a God who is worthy of any and every sacrifice. Have we become those who try to draw people by worldly means? Are we reversing the message Jesus gave the rich young ruler, in effect saying, "You don't have to sacrifice anything, Jesus will take what you can give Him?"

Here are five practical questions to test your level of sacrifice:

1. Does God get "the best" of my money?

2. Does my schedule reflect that seeking God is by far my number one goal?

3. Do I expend more energy seeking God or pursuing other things?

4. Am I sacrificing my skills, resources, time, and money to seek God first?

5. Am I giving God leftovers or the best of the life He has given me?

What if you set the goal of writing your biggest monthly check to God's work? What if the first hour(s) of the day were set aside for God and Him alone? What if the first and best expenditure of your mental and physical energy was in "seeking God first?" If you have children, what sacrifice do they see that you have clearly made to pursue God first? Take a ruthless inventory of this simple question: "What has it truly cost me to pursue God?"

In the American church today, we have so lowered the bar that I fear our Christianity is not even the real thing. Like watered-down tea or coffee, we have lost our flavor and the very essence of what we were meant to be. Our dilemma can be compared with receiving a vaccine. It gives you just enough of the sickness to keep you from getting the disease itself. Have we been inoculated with just enough Jesus to keep us from getting the real thing? There is a remedy—but it will cost you everything. Yet when you see the surpassing glory of Jesus, no sacrifice will seem too great. You will gladly pay it with your very life!

The late German pastor Dietrich Bonhoeffer, who has been popularized by Eric Metaxas' excellent biography, said that "When Christ calls a man, He bids them come and die." If this sounds altogether ruthless, and less than biblical, listen to Jesus' very own words:

> "If anyone would come after me, let him deny himself and take up his cross and follow me. For whoever would save his life will lose it, but whoever loses his life for my sake will find it" (Matt. 16:24-25)

> "Whoever loves father or mother more than me is not worthy of me, and whoever loves son or daughter more than me is not worthy of me. And whoever does not take his cross and follow me is not worthy of me" (Matt. 10:37-38)

> "So therefore, any one of you who does not renounce all that he has cannot be my disciple" (Luke 14:33)

DECADES

Imagine that when Mary Anne and I stood at the altar to marry on July 20, 1985 my handwritten vows had gone something like this:

> *"My dear Mary Anne, I commit my life to you for the next year. If things go well, I will commit a while longer. No long-term commitments or sacrifices will be guaranteed. I will take it day by day and see how it goes."*

Do you think that would have flown? I know it would not! Yet many pursue Jesus in much the same way. We give "seeking God" a try. We test-drive God to see whether we like Him. But born-again believers have entered into a covenant with God far more enduring than the sacred vows of marriage. You may have had a past season of intense seeking of God that has now grown cold. If so, now is the time to set your heart to "love God" and to make your true life goal simply to "seek His face." Understand that this endeavor will take a commitment of decade upon decade of going hard after God. It's not a forty-day pursuit, or a year's commitment, or even a few years' push to know Him. Don't evaluate the results for at least five years. This is a long-term goal that is fulfilled daily. You are setting your heart on a daily, monthly, yearly, and literally decades-long journey of seeking to know Him.

I often think about a favorite song our church sang years ago, Tommy Walker's Never Gonna Stop. Part of it goes:

When the last day comes and goes and time will be no more

I'll be praising you

A thousand years from now before Your throne of grace and power

I'll be praising You

These lyrics resonate in the depths of my heart. I know what I will be doing a thousand years from now: I'll be caught up in unending, ever-increasing, joy-filled worship of God who will be manifest in my very presence. I will be awestruck every second that eternity moves ahead. Not only will I never be bored, but I will be stunned as I am transformed from "glory to glory" in all consuming worship of Jesus! The God who will be altogether worthy, mesmerizing, and ravishing in heaven is the same God that you and I get to spend time with right now. He's exactly the same!

Paul warns us that the "the god of this world has blinded the minds of the unbelievers, to keep them from seeing the light of the gospel of the glory of Christ, who is the image of God" (2 Cor. 4:4). Do you see what unbelievers can't see? They can't see the glory of God in the face of Christ. But we can! "For God who said, 'Let light shine out of darkness,' has shone in our hearts to give the light of the knowledge of the glory of God in the face of Jesus Christ," says 2 Corinthians 4:6. Our eyes have been opened to see the glory of God in Jesus Christ. Jesus is the way to seek, see, and experience the Father.

How do we grow, see, and experience more of the glory of God in the face of Christ? I've learned over the years that this pursuit is daily, difficult, and often two steps forward and one step back. The key is to not get discouraged and not to give up. Don't compare yourself with others. Seek God more deeply than you ever have. That's growth. Do you love Jesus more than you did last year? Does He have more of your heart, soul, mind, and strength than He did two years ago? If your answer is "yes," rejoice and ask for more. If not, repent and quickly return, pressing into God for more.

In order to maintain a life-long pursuit of God, it is essential to repent quickly and move relationally back to God. I learned this lesson from two Catholic Christians who have changed the face of modern Christianity. One you will know and the other you must get to know! Martin Luther, the father of the Protestant reformation, nailed ninety-five theses to the door of the Wittenberg Cathedral on October 31, 1517. I have read his list and have had trouble making sense of much of it, to be honest. The first statement, however, has revolutionized my life:

> "Our Lord and Master Jesus Christ...willed that the whole life of believers should be repentance."

That means that I don't wait until the end of the day, the month, or the year to repent and turn back to Jesus. The daily movement of my heart is to continually turn back to Jesus, over and over again. This is the life of the believer, a life of continual repentance. Remember, repentance is simply turning from lesser things to focus on Jesus Christ. Repentance is not only a good thing, but the primary way we move toward a life of seeking God's face.

The other, lesser-known Catholic Christian from the 1600s is Brother Lawrence. The author of the simple, motivational book *The Practice of the Presence of God*, Brother Lawrence was not a monk or a priest. He was an ordinary layperson, a lowly cook at a Carmelite Monastery in France. Yet his book has done more to encourage true seekers of God than almost any book in history. I've had the privilege of reading it several times, and have been transformed by the following the principles which guided Brother Lawrence:

- Never stop your conversation with Jesus, no matter what you are doing. Brother Lawrence said he virtually had a forty-year conversation with Jesus.

- When you find that you have drifted from Jesus, simply repent quickly and return to the conversation with Him.

- Refuse to allow yourself to get caught up in the fact that you drifted or fell; simply repent quickly and return to Jesus. He accepts you fully, and is excited to continue the conversation.

- Never separate work or hardship from your conversation with Jesus. There is no separation. All events are merely different God-ordained settings for your ongoing relationship with Jesus.

One final word on setting your heart and mind to seek God for decades: what you sow now you will reap ten years from now. This is good news for those who set their heart to seek God daily, moment by moment, and bad news for those who are sowing to the lust of the eyes, the lust of the flesh, and the pride of life (1 John 2:16). Galatians 6:7 says it like this:

> "Do not be deceived: God is not mocked, for whatever one sows, that will he also reap. For the one who sows to his own flesh will from the flesh reap corruption, but the one who sow to the Spirit will from the Spirit reap eternal life."

The gravest danger I see facing Christians in modern America is that we have separated our lives into the unbiblical categories of "sacred" and "secular" activities. We have our church friends and experiences and then we have our work and hobby friends. Sadly, the two lives rarely meet. This is sin, and it is dangerously destructive for those who long to see God fully. Jesus must reign over all areas of our lives. He is the reason we go to work, get married, have children, and enjoy hobbies. The true seeker of God will repent of this secularization of life. There is no such divide. God is to be the main character of our lives, the center of all our actions, thoughts, and intentions, in all spheres. This will lead you to the joy of all joys—knowing Jesus Christ as the passionate love of your entire life!

SMALL GROUP QUESTIONS

1. If following Jesus cost you everything, would it still be worth it? Explain.

2. How do your affections, schedules, and balance sheets reveal whether God is first in your life?

3. RECAPTURE: If you received a personal letter from Jesus in the mail today and He said you had "abandoned your first love", what specifically would He be talking about?

4. HOLY SPIRIT: Why is Luke 11:13 the most amazing promise ever, one that changes everything for believers? What will you do in response to it?

5. LONG HOURS: Are you willing to take the two-hour-a-week prayer room challenge for the next year? Why or why not?

6. SACRIFICE: Should following Jesus cost us everything (Matt. 16:24-25, 10:37-38, Luke 14:33)?

7. DECADES: How do you think the following level of commitment would go over in your marriage?

"My dear, I commit my life to you for the next year. If things go well I will commit a while longer. No long term commitments or sacrifices will be guaranteed. I will take it day by day and see how it goes."

Why do we settle for this kind of commitment to Christ?

REVIVAL CRY ACTION STEP

Commit to two hours a week in the prayer room, with accountability.

CHAPTER 6

YOUR MOST IMPORTANT GIFT: REPENTANCE

"If my people, who are called by My name, will humble themselves, and pray and seek my face and turn from their wicked ways..."
- 2 Chronicles 7:14

It was in the 1980s: I was a brand-new Christian and contemporary Christian music was emerging on the scene. The artist was Scott Wesley Brown and his song went like this:

Fools who march to win the right to justify their sin

Every nation that has fallen, has fallen from within

That's all I remember, but that's all I need to remember. The danger of sin is incalculable. The only thing that can exponentially magnify sin's danger is when we fight to justify it. Seeking to "okay" our sin is the most grievous shame ever endured by the church. God is not first and foremost speaking to the lost about their sin in 2 Chronicles 7:14—that's normal behavior for them. He is speaking to His people about that which kills revival, joy, passion for Jesus, and destinies!

TWEET: @Trey_Kent

We must breathe the air of heaven more than the air of culture in order to be change agents for Christ

The normal state of the church should be revival—fully alive in God. Remember, revival is endeavoring to love God with all your heart, soul, mind, and strength, and loving everyone else as much as we love ourselves. If that standard seems unattainable, God has great news: Jesus has promised to transform His much-loved bride into a pure and passionate lover worthy of all His affection. Ephesians 5:25-27 says:

"Christ loved the church and gave himself up for her, that he might sanctify her, having cleansed her by the washing of water with the word, so that he might present the church to himself in splendor, without spot or wrinkle or any such thing, that she might be holy and without blemish."

This is the end state of the church. Now, let's look at how God gets us there!

THE FATHER'S ROLE

The key to understanding the need for us to "turn from our wicked ways" is rooted in who God is. He is holy! In Isaiah 6, the prophet repeats the seraphs' constant chant, "Holy, Holy, Holy." In the Hebrew language, an important point is emphasized through repetition. No other attribute of God has been highlighted in this same way as in this three-fold proclamation. To say God is holy is to say not only that He is absolutely and infinitely pure, but that He is categorically different from everyone else: He is totally other. This reality is mind-boggling for creatures like us who breathe air, walk on the ground, and know little more than things that the senses can experience. God's true nature, in His infinite holiness, is totally foreign to us.

In his *Attributes of God* study, A.W. Tozer says that the problem between us and God is dissimilarity. We feel distant from Him, not because we are far from him in distance, but because we are unlike Him in character. Sin—both the kind we inherited and the type we have committed—is what creates this fog of separation that covers the beauty of God's holiness. Revival occurs when God moves mightily in the heart of a believer so that he or she can not only rejoice in a holy God, but can see the beauty of His holiness as a pursuit worthy all of his heart, soul, mind, and strength. Going into the holy of holies becomes an awesome privilege that consumes the dross in our lives. For a vivid picture of this revelation of God, let's note how He showed Himself to Moses.

"The Lord descended in the cloud and stood with him there, and proclaimed the name of the LORD, a God merciful and gracious, slow to anger, and abounding in steadfast love and faithfulness, keeping steadfast love for thousands, forgiving iniquity and transgression and sin, but who will by no means clear the guilty, visiting the iniquity of the fathers on the children and the children's children, to the third and fourth generation" (Exod. 34:6-7)

There are five revelations from this passage:

1. God is full of mercy, which is His goodness to those who are afflicted.

2. God is gracious, which is His goodness to those who deserve only punishment.

3. God is slow to anger.

4. God is overflowing in faithful love.

5. God forgives those who repent, and punishes those who maintain guilt through refusing to repent.

As God proclaims His name to Moses, we see clearly that He loves to reveal His goodness to those afflicted. This is a standard operating procedure for God's daily work on planet earth. God is full of grace toward us who deserve only hell. That's an astonishing thought. I remember how shocked I was when, watching a live stream from the IHOP-KC prayer room, I heard Misty Edwards, one of the worship leaders, sing a song that said:

> *You owe me nothing. I deserve hell, but You've given me mercy.*

As she repeated these lines, they forged an indelible groove in my conscience. Believe me, after hearing that for ten straight minutes you get the point—God has given us what we don't deserve! In the declaration of His name, God declares Himself slow to anger. David affirms that God does not treat us as our sins deserve, but forgives us. God is overflowing in consistent love. Here's the key to understanding this passage: God is merciful, gracious, slow to anger, and faithful in love to those who repent. Those who do, He gladly forgives iniquity (rebellion), transgression (offense), and sin (missing the mark). Those who refuse to repent, and so forfeit His grace, are put in a different category. They are called the "guilty," and are not only punished personally for their sin, but their punishment reaches down to the third and fourth generation. This is a strong admonition to deal with our sin now!

What a gracious God. What an astonishing truth. If we repent of sin, transgression, and iniquity then we are no longer called guilty. But those who retain their sin are forced to fend for themselves. And there is no defense against the all-consuming holiness of God which lays us bare with nowhere to hide. The grace of God has two powerful effects on the life of the believer. Grace causes us to:

- Be made alive with Christ (Eph. 2:5)

- Say "no" to ungodliness and "yes" to righteousness (Titus 2:11-12)

The danger today is that the often-preached "cheap grace" message results in people remaining in sin willfully because they believe the grace of

God will cover it anyway. That's when the terrifying warning of Hebrews 10:26 rises up:

> "For if we go on sinning deliberately after receiving the knowledge of the truth, there no longer remains a sacrifice for sins."

In other words, don't take grace for granted. Grace is God's gift to cover sin, but equally important is God's grace to empower us not to sin.

🐦 TWEET: @OneCry

If our faith looks more like the culture than the Bible, there's a problem. How much of YOUR OWN Christianity is cultural vs. Biblical?

The normal and natural state of the believer is walking in a revived or alive state with God. Sin is the enemy of this. Sin is not only shameful and disgraceful to our new identity in Christ, but it's now foreign to our very nature. Paul urges the Romans to "consider yourselves dead to sin and alive to Christ" (Rom. 6:11). In other words, sin is never to be enabled by us because it is revolting to our new nature, which is filled with the Holy Spirit. That's why the Bible warns believers not to "grieve the Holy Spirit of God, by whom you were sealed for the day of redemption" (Eph. 4:32). Paul teaches the church at Corinth, even with all their problems and issues:

> "Therefore, if anyone is in Christ, he is a new creation. The old has passed away; behold the new has come" (2 Cor. 5:17)

Paul tells the church at Galatia:

> "But far be it from me to boast except in the cross of our Lord Jesus Christ, by which the world has been crucified to me, and I to the world. For neither circumcision counts for anything, nor uncircumcision, but a new creation" (Gal. 6:14-15)

Before we proceed any further, let's define sin so we can know what it means to "forsake our wicked ways." The Bible teaches that "sin is lawlessness" (1 John 3:4), or breaking God's Word (law). This clearly and squarely fits into our definition of revival as loving God with our all, and loving our neighbor as ourselves. Let's revisit those passages that define what true, ongoing revival is.

> "And he said to him, 'You shall love the Lord your God with all your heart and with all your soul and with all your mind. This is the great and first commandment. And a second is like it: You shall love your neighbor as yourself. On these

two commandments, depend all the Law and the Prophets'" (Matt. 22:37-40)

Sin, at its core, occurs anytime we don't love God with all our heart, soul, mind, and strength, and fail to love our neighbor as ourselves. Do you see how often we sin? Matthew 22:40 shows clearly that all the law and the prophets are summed up in these two commands. So, the enemy of revival is anything that hinders us from loving God with our whole heart and from loving our neighbors as much as we love ourselves. Do you see it? Satan's number one tool for stopping revival is to get the church off-track from the life-transforming pursuit of loving God and loving others. Selfishness or pride is the root of all sin, thinking that we are going to be fulfilled outside of God.

Our problem is not new. It goes all the way back to our first parents. God provided Adam and Eve with a perfect environment in which to fulfill the first commandment of loving God wholeheartedly, and the second commandment of loving one another. Satan came and used pride or selfishness to draw Eve, then Adam, into sin. Sin was and is missing the mark of loving God and others. Satan's lure was to tempt Adam and Eve to try to rule their own lives by obtaining the knowledge of both good and evil. Satan tricked this first couple into becoming their own gods and ruling their own lives. This is the heart of sin. The song of sin is, "It's all about me, my, and mine." It diametrically opposes revival, which is loving God and loving others. To love God is to obey His commandments.

JESUS' ROLE

Our hope and ability to "turn from our wicked ways" is not in a plan, but a person—Jesus Christ. At the heart of our freedom from sin's dominion is the miracle of our identification with Christ's life, death, burial, and resurrection. Our hope for freedom is not imaginary or questionable. It is a reality that is found only "in Christ." Consider the stunning hope of being 'In Christ."

SEVEN WAYS WE ARE IDENTIFIED WITH CHRIST

1. I was in Jesus Christ as He lived my perfect life for me (Rom. 8:3-4)

2. I was in Jesus Christ as He died my death for me (Gal. 2:20)

3. I was in Jesus Christ as He was buried for my sins (Rom. 6:4, Col. 2:12)

4. I was in Christ as He was raised from the dead (Rom. 6:4,

Col. 2:12)

5.   I am seated with Jesus Christ as He now sits in heavenly places (Eph. 2:6)

6.   I am currently one in spirit with Christ Jesus (1 Cor. 6:17)

7.   I am currently following in Christ's victory (2 Cor. 2:14)

Sin can never be dealt with by any fleshly or human means, nor by trying to clean up our lives or seeking to obey the law. The Bible reveals that the "one who sows to his flesh will from the flesh reap corruption" (Gal. 6:8). We cannot keep the law in ourselves because all the flesh can produce is more flesh and death (John 3:6, Rom. 8:3-4). No one has the inherent will-power needed to overcome sin, because our hearts are sin factories (Jer. 17:9).

The only remedy for defeating sin is, by faith, to trust Christ as our victory, our hope, and our life. Putting away our wicked ways is not a human endeavor—it is through Christ we put off the old nature and put on the new nature (Col. 3:9-10).

Our rightful victory over sin, Satan, and the world is founded and grounded in the finished work of Christ. Jesus lived our perfect life. Jesus died, killing our old life. The old us was buried with Christ in the tomb. The new us arose from the dead with Christ and is as alive as the resurrected Christ is at the right hand of the Father, right now. As Jesus ascended into heaven and is seated next to His Father, we ascended with Him and are currently seated with Him.

Jesus Christ poured the Holy Spirit into our hearts to make us one with Himself. He will never see us apart from Himself again because we are now one spirit with Him. Jesus is now leading us in His victory. We win over sin, evil, and lust because Jesus has already defeated all these enemies. We win because we are "in Christ." He is our victor!

How does walking in this victory practically work? Daily we are taught by Jesus to pray the truths of the Lord's Prayer. We cry out, "lead us not into temptation, but deliver us from evil." When a temptation arises, we agree with God and state that we are dead to sin but alive to Christ. To resist sin, we go to Christ. We celebrate His love and affection for us, and stand in Him. When we fail, we quickly repent and return to fellowship with Christ. As God reveals areas of compromise and wickedness in our lives, we agree with God and turn from those deadly traps, gladly giving them up for new life in Christ

🐦**TWEET:** Pray Always! @erotao

Prayer will make a man cease from sin, or sin will entice a man to cease from prayer. ~ John Bunyan

THE HOLY SPIRIT'S ROLE

Many today remain ignorant of the third person of the Trinity: God, the Holy Spirit. Some have erroneously called the Holy Spirit an "it" or a force. The Holy Spirit is fully God and is a person in the same manner as Father God and Jesus. The Holy Spirit in His very essence is equal to Father God and to Jesus Christ. Jesus told His disciples that it was better that He went away—to be crucified, buried, resurrected, and ascend to Heaven—so He could send another "Comforter" to be with us forever (John 14-16). The Holy Spirit's ministry in the believer is vast and essential to our "turning from our wicked ways."

There are five key ways the Holy Spirit enables us to defeat sin. He:

1. Fills us with power (Acts 1:8)

2. Lead us into all truth (John 14-16)

3. Convicts us of sin (John 16:8-9)

4. Convicts us of righteousness (John 16:8,10)

5. Convicts us of judgment (John 16:8, 11)

There is not a more dramatic demonstration of the Holy Spirit's ability to transform a person than the New Testament's description of Peter, the fisherman chosen to be a disciple. He was a verbal man who often made incredibly amazing declarations—which were followed shortly by equally stupid proclamations. In one account, Peter is enlightened by Father God to see that Jesus is indeed the long-awaited Messiah. Then, a few short verses later, Peter is used by Satan to rebuke Jesus and to try to dissuade Him from going to the cross. Peter's lowest moment has to be after Jesus' arrest in the palace garden. Previously, Peter had promised to die with Jesus. Now, we see the weakness of human flesh at its worst. Not only does Peter refuse to die with Jesus, he publicly denies knowing Him, three times. This tragic event recorded in the gospel accounts shows clearly how impossible it is for us to obey God in our own strength, no matter how much willpower we try to exert.

Peter, like every human, was powerless to change himself. He faced some dark days after his denial, but better times were on the horizon. Jesus met with the disciples for forty days, revealing Himself and teaching them. The Living Word, Jesus, who wrote the scriptures, was now teaching them.

Yet, this was not enough. At the end of the forty-day study, upon His ascension to heaven, Jesus commanded the disciples to go and wait for the outpouring of the Holy Spirit. The disciples once again met in the upper room, locked down, out of fear of the religious leaders. Yet, gloriously, they began to seek God for ten straight days and nights. Then "the day" was revealed. Acts 2:1-14 tells how:

> "When the day of Pentecost arrived, they were all together in one place. And suddenly there came from heaven a sound like a mighty rushing wind, and it filled the entire house where they were sitting. And divided tongues as of fire appeared to them and rested on each of them. And they all were filled with the Holy Spirit and began to speak in other tongues as the Spirit gave them utterance…And at this sound the multitude came together…all were amazed and perplexed…others mocking said, 'They are filled with new wine.' But Peter, standing with the eleven, lifted up his voice and addressed them."

Peter was a new man. The old Peter caved under the pressure of mocking. Now, filled with the Holy Spirit, he preached a powerful and confrontational message to people from all over the world. He had denied Christ to a slave girl, but now he boldly proclaimed Him publicly and three thousand people were saved. What made the difference? One person; Peter was now filled with the power of the Holy Spirit. The wickedness of self-preservation, selfishness, and denial of Christ was replaced as he exchanged his old life for the infinite power of the Holy Spirit. We can also experience the power of the Holy Spirit. Peter teaches in his first sermon in Acts 2:38-39:

> "Repent and be baptized every one of you in the name of Jesus Christ for the forgiveness of your sins, and you will receive the gift of the Holy Spirit. For the promise is for you and for your children and for all who are far off, everyone whom the Lord God calls to himself."

Not only does the Holy Spirit empower us, but He leads us into all truth. The Holy Spirit is called "the Spirit of Truth" (John 16:13). Many times we tend to make a distinction between "Word" people and "Spirit" people. This is unnecessary and ultimately unbiblical. The Spirit of God and the Word of God are perfectly unified in every way. The Spirit of God will reveal what the Bible means. It is impossible to "turn from our wicked ways" without both the truth of the Word of God and the revelation of the Holy Spirit. Through the Word we begin to see the vast evil that we have embraced, tolerated, or celebrated. As we see evil from God's perspective we begin to put aside evil ways through repentance and confession of sin.

The Holy Spirit is our teacher. In fact, 1 John 2:27 tells us:

> "But the anointing that you received from him abides in you, and you have no need that anyone teaches you. But His anointing teaches you about everything, and is true, and is no lie—just as it has taught you, abide him."

As we listen to and follow the "anointing" of the Holy Spirit within, He will teach us. This is good news. We love to listen to teachers, preachers, and those who lead Bible studies. They are a necessary part of maturing the body of Christ (Eph. 4:11-13), but don't settle for human teachers alone when you can have the Holy Spirit teach you. The Holy Spirit's teaching is essential to break free from evil. John 8:32 says, "You will know the truth, and the truth will set you free," while John 17:17 says, "Your Word is truth." Holiness, or being set apart for God and for His purposes, comes as the Holy Spirit teaches us the Word of God.

Jesus teaches His disciples the importance of the Holy Spirit's ministry on the earth in John 16:7-11:

> "Nevertheless, I tell you the truth: it is to your advantage that I go away, for if I do not go away, the Helper will not come to you. And when he comes, he will convict the world concerning sin and righteousness and judgment: concerning sin, because they do not believe in me; concerning righteousness, because I go to the Father, and you will see me no longer; concerning judgment because the ruler of this world is judged."

🐦 TWEET: @OneCry

Revival is falling in love with Jesus all over again. - Vance Havner // How would you rate your love for Jesus today?

The Holy Spirit convicts the world and the church of sin. This is a great gift. Revival is prevented in our hearts because we won't deal with our sin. As I read about revivals old and new, one key factor remains consistent: sin must be dealt with. Why do you think it has been hundreds of years since America has experienced widespread revival?

I believe the reason is because sin has become so vague and relative that no one believes they need to repent. In the midst of this deception, the Bible is crystal clear that the Holy Spirit is convicting. The problem of minimizing sin is not new. Stephen rebuked the Jews in his day:

"You stiff-necked people, uncircumcised in heart and ears, you always resist the Holy Spirit. As your fathers did, so do you" (Acts 7:51)

Today we resist the conviction of the Holy Spirit in many ways. Stop now and ask the Lord where you may have been resisting the Spirit of God's conviction that is sent to lead you out of darkness and into a deeper love for Jesus. The Bible warns "having itching ears they will accumulate for themselves teachers to suit their own passions" (2 Tim 4:3). We are also warned against changing our theology to protect the sinful lifestyle we lead. It's commonplace to hear Americans say that the Bible is passé, or they reject the Old Testament and maintain animosity against the teachings of Paul. Peter Himself recognized that Paul's letters were equal with Scripture (2 Pet. 3:15-16)! We must bow the knee, not rearrange truth to fit our lifestyles.

🐦 TWEET: @John Piper

How I stay a Christian. "I will put the fear of me in their hearts, that they may not turn from me." Jeremiah 32:40

The chief sin the Holy Spirit is sent to confront is unbelief in Jesus. True faith results in a clean break with the old life, and enables believers to grow more like Jesus in the midst of our struggles. Faith in Christ is the key to growth, maturity, and becoming Christ-like. The sin that will ultimately condemn sinners— eternally that is—is refusing to believe in Christ. "Easy believism" or mere mental assent to God will never save. True salvation results from faith that leads to forsaking all our ways and all our thoughts in exchange for Christ, His ways, and His thoughts (Isa. 55:8).

The Holy Spirit also convicts us of righteousness. The Bible gives the meaning of righteousness. It's not good works alone. The Holy Spirit will convict of righteousness because Jesus goes to the Father: our only acceptance before Father God comes in Jesus Christ alone. He is our righteousness (2 Cor. 5:21). Jesus being our righteousness, both in heaven and in our hearts, enables us to live righteously through the Spirit's power within. God is a righteous God, and only those who are robed in Christ's perfect righteousness will enjoy both heaven's joy in the future and earthly joy now as we rest in His finished work. We walk righteously because Jesus is our righteousness. The Holy Spirit not only convicts us of our sin, but He convicts us of our need for Christ's righteousness. An effective way to pray regularly is to verbalize the following: "Jesus, I thank you that you have made me totally acceptable to God. Now, please send Your Spirit to empower me to live righteously."

The Holy Spirit not only convicts us of sin and righteousness, but also of judgment. Once again, this statement is followed by unexpected words. Jesus teaches us that ultimately we want to avoid being judged with Satan. All those who reject Christ will be judged with him. The Holy Spirit is warning unbelievers to repent, and believers not to engage in behaviors that are satanic in origin and that will ultimately receive the wrath of God. Those who are not "known" by Christ will suffer eternally for the sin of partnering with Satan, the one who sought to be worshiped in heaven and even now fights to steal glory from the one true God. It is so vital to holiness and forsaking our wicked ways that we are sensitive to the Spirit's convictions on a moment-by-moment basis and that we repent quickly. We can then move back into a joy-filled relationship with God.

OBEDIENCE

As we've seen, all sin is refusing to love God with all our heart, soul, mind, and strength, or refusing to love our neighbor as ourselves. Jesus teaches this same truth in John 14:23-24:

> "If anyone loves me, he will keep my word, and my Father will love him, and will come to him and make our home with him. Whoever does not love me does not keep my words. And the word that you hear is not mine but the Father's who sent me."

It is impossible to define true love for Jesus apart from obedience. In the modern church, though, many reject the idea that obedience is essential to verify true love. Are we going to stand with Jesus or modern teachers?

In fact, we read in the Bible that we are to both know God and to obey God. These two pursuits are inseparable. It is impossible to love God and not seek to obey Him. That does not mean we will be perfect in our obedience. So thank God for 1 John 1:9-2:1:

> "If we confess our sins, he is faithful and just to forgive us our sins and to cleanse us from all unrighteousness. If we say we have not sinned, we make him a liar, and his word is not in us. My little children, I am writing to you so that you may not sin. But if anyone does sin, we have an advocate with the Father, Jesus Christ the righteous."

The point is clear: we will sin. We will fall down. We will mess up—at times royally. But we refuse to justify our sin, make excuses for our sin, or call it a mistake. Those who love God and seek to obey Him call sin what it is, and refuse to whitewash that which Jesus paid so dearly to heal. We have so much freedom because God has forgiven us already. We confess our sins not to be loved by God—Jesus loved us while we were yet sinners. As believers we confess our sin to restore our relationship with God. We repent to remove the distance, or the dissimilarity between us and God.

Take some time to sit before God and ask Him where you need to repent of your wicked ways. Jesus is your advocate; you will not be rejected. Do not allow un-dealt with sin to put walls between you and the Father. It's not worth it. King David, who was an adulterer, murderer, and liar, was called by God a man after His own heart. Why? Because David trusted God's character and regularly said;

> "Search me O God and know my heart; test me and know
> my anxious thoughts. See if there is any offensive way in me
> and lead me in the way everlasting" (Ps. 139:23-24)

Go after God's heart with the same fervency as David. You will never regret it. Wickedness is standing in the way of revival. Refuse to allow your heart to be torn by sin's ravishing. Take Tozer's advice and "Deal thoroughly and honestly with sin." This will ensure that you not only experience God's best, but that you are an agent of change to spread the fire of God throughout the earth.

TWEET: @Trey_Kent

Fear of God is essential to boldly fulfilling the purpose for which you were created by Jesus and for Jesus! See Isaiah 33:5-6

THE EXCHANGED LIFE

What We Give Up		What we get in return
Our sin	2 Cor. 5:21	Christ's righteousness
Wrath of God	Rom. 5:1	Peace with God
Condemnation (hell)	Eph. 2:6, 19	Father's House (heaven)
Death	Gal. 2:20	Life
The Old Nature	2 Cor. 5:17	The New Nature
Law	Rom. 7:4-6	Grace
Our Weakness	2 Cor. 12:9-10	His Strength
Our Impurity	Heb. 10:21-22	His Purity
Eternal Wickedness	Eph. 1:4	Holiness of God
Self-sufficiency	Isa. 40:31	God's Power
Hostility	Eph. 2:14	Peace
Defeat	1 Cor. 15:57	Victory
Sorrow	John 15:11	Joy

from www.exchangedlife.org

SMALL GROUP QUESTIONS

1.   How and why do we justify our sin?

2.   "The normal and natural state of the believer is walking in a revived or alive state with God." Do you agree or disagree? Why?

3.   Sin kills revival (loving God and others). How have you seen this to be true in your own life?

4.   What strikes you most in Exodus 34:6-7? Why?

5.   Do you embrace God's holiness or run from it? Explain

6.   How does understanding the seven ways we are identified with Christ help us live free from sin and pursue God?

7.   How do you identify with Peter both before Pentecost and afterward?

8.   How can you grow in seeing conviction and repentance as a good thing?

9.   Do you think most Christians agree that to "love God is to seek to obey Him?"

10. What is your biggest take-home from this chapter?

REVIVAL CRY ACTION ITEM

Set a weekly meeting with God where you ask Him to reveal what sin(s) are stopping revival in you.

CHAPTER 7

YOUR MOST IMPORTANT PROMISE: REVIVAL

"If my people, who are called by My name, will humble themselves, and pray and seek my face and turn from their wicked ways then I will hear from heaven, and I will forgive their sin and will heal their land."
- 2 Chronicles 7:14

Revival bursts forth when the Holy Spirit is poured out in such a way that love for God floods the church and contagiously overflows into the city streets. I have literally dreamed about this. In my dream, the streets of Austin were filled, packed like nothing I'd ever seen, with worshipers publicly rejoicing in God.   Acts 2:17 declares:

> "And in the last days it shall be, God declares, that I will pour out my Spirit on all flesh, and your sons and your daughters shall prophesy, and your young men shall see visions, and your old men shall dream dreams."

This is the revival we are contending for in prayer. God has promised it, we are praying, and revival is coming. Like me, you have probably never truly experienced a widespread revival, not a true revival of biblical proportions. Today, the word "revival" has been reduced to extended meetings at local churches featuring outside speakers who lead nightly gatherings. This is not what we are contending for in prayer! We are contending for a move of the Holy Spirit so powerful that all segments of the city— young and old, rich and poor, east and west, black and white, Christian and non-Christian—are transformed by a mighty move of God.

🐦 TWEET: George Whitefield @WhitefiledG

"America was born in a revival of religion. Back of that revival were John Wesley, George Whitefield and Francis Asbury." Calvin Coolidge

Do you truly believe it could happen? I am certain of it! Is this a pipe dream that is only distracting us from the current pain in our lives? Not a chance. Is it truly in God's heart to bring this kind of historic event to the cities of America? Yes, He promised!

In my dream I see revival hitting Austin so powerfully that the churches can no longer contain the masses of people desiring to worship God. Worship spills over into the streets, and this move of God is led by a new and more radical generation. Older leaders make way for younger ones to pastor this move of God as it spreads deeper into the next generation. The revival will look different and feel different than anything we've seen before. It will be exhilarating and challenging, joyous and stretching. That's all I see for now. But, better than my dream interpretation, let's look at what God Word reveals about what historic revival looks like when it hits a city.

The first New Testament revival was called Pentecost.

PRE-REVIVAL ESSENTIALS

Before we jump into the powerful Jerusalem revival that began in Acts 2 and spread worldwide, we need to consider some pre-revival essentials. These conditions must be in place before revival hits.

We can find the criteria in 2 Chronicles 7:14:

> "If my people who are called by my name humble themselves and pray and seek my face and turn from their wicked ways, then I will hear from heaven and I will forgive their sin and heal their land."

In this passage we find five conditions that must be met, along with one hope-giving promise:

- Condition 1: Revival begins with the people of God.

- Condition 2: Revival comes to a people who have humbled themselves.

- Condition 3: Revival is given to a people who have contended in prayer.

- Condition 4: Revival is poured out on a people who have seriously sought after God.

- Condition 5: Revival will come to a people who have turned from their wicked ways.

   Promise: *God will hear their prayer, forgive their sin, and heal their land.*

This is not meant to be a formula, for there are none that can be applied to revival. But the Bible does give conditions that must be met before revival will come. Think with me about your local church. Would you characterize it as being full of a people who are humble, praying, seeking God, and turning from wickedness? No, I wouldn't describe my church exactly like that, either. But, I do see a remnant, a small group of emerging revivalists hungry for nothing but God and fed up with business as usual. I believe this small group of contenders can lead the way in humility, prayer, seeking God's face, and repentance. They can ignite and spread the fires of revival within families, churches, neighborhoods, and cities.

🐦 TWEET: @Prayer_Coach

At the heart of every revival is the spirit of prayer. - Arthur Wallis

It's not uncommon in church history for revivals to begin with only one or two people and result in changed nations. What if you decided not to be the judge of what you like or don't like in the local church, but forged ahead humbly, prayerfully seeking after God's heart, and repenting of your own sin? What if you began to lead others to pursue the same missionary lifestyle? Revival must begin in me: I need it most! I have no rocks to throw at the church. I am the one most in need. Revival will not begin as I tell others that they need to be revived, but as I seriously humble myself to pray like never before, to pursue the face of God in unprecedented ways, and to repent more deeply than ever. Revival begins as you and I say to God: "I am so sorry. It's not okay how I've lived, prayed, sought your face, or left wickedness un-dealt with in my own heart. Send revival, and begin with me!"

🐦 TWEET: @Trey_Kent

40 days of Bible study w/ the resurrected Christ was not enough...the disciples needed the outpouring of the Holy Spirit to change the world

THE ACTS 2 MODEL

As the disciples were holed up in the upper room, seeking God for ten days and nights, He was about to pour out a historic revival, one so massive it is still the standard for all moves of God. Here are the key words I would use to describe the move of God in Acts 2:1-14: suddenly, loud, fiery, miraculous, unprecedented, contagious, misunderstood, unstoppable. The disciples' prayer meeting was interrupted by a powerful sound like a rushing wind that filled the entire house. Tongues of fire rested on each one and they began to speak in languages they didn't know. God miraculously caused this outpouring of the Holy Spirit to draw the multitudes that were in Jerusalem for the Jewish festival of Pentecost.

These Jews from around the world began to hear these uneducated Galileans praising God fluently and perfectly in their native languages. This caused quite a stir; some mocked and claimed the disciples were drunk. Something like this has never happened at my church, and it would definitely be opposed by some. What about at yours?

I hope this brief description of the first fourteen verses of Acts 2 helps you understand that revival will come in dramatic and unexpected ways. I fear that the modern church wants a neat, clean, and un-messy revival. I've yet to read about one like that. In fact, I was amused to read that Andrew Murray, the South African pastor and leader in the 1800s, who had learned about revival at his father's knee, almost missed it when it came unexpectedly and dramatically to his youth group. He thought the uncontrollable crying out to God by the young people was out of order, so he shut down the meeting. But God was not finished. The next time the youth gathered, God once again poured out His Spirit and they responded again in loud outbursts. God had to speak to Murray and show him that he was trying to shut down the very move of God that he had been contending for all his life.

When revival hits, it will be uncontrollable, uncontainable, and unstoppable. The unorthodox nature of the events will stretch even those of us who have been looking for it. God will use people we never expected, and people will act in ways we don't understand. He will also pass by others whom we thought He would and should use. And yes, some will respond in a fleshly and fake manner in the midst of revival, trying to manufacture something God is not doing. The actions of Ananias and Sapphira, in Acts 5, show that such responses will be a part of any true move of God.

In America's First Great Awakening, God moved in such out-of-the-ordinary ways that Jonathan Edwards, the great pastor and leader in the awakening, spent much of his time defending the revival against pastors' and other believers' attacks. From the extensive reading I have done of past revivals, it is awesome, but not neat. Revival is passionate, but not always pretty. Revival is full of God's power, but is very uncomfortable. When revival hits, the churches will not all be gathered in one place, singing sweet songs, in perfect unity with no distractions. The opposite may be true. As revival hits—at least, historically speaking—the power of God brings opposition very much like what we see in the book of Acts. Religious people are always the first to oppose a move of God.

The revival in Acts resulted in the death of the Apostle James and the newly appointed leader, Stephen. Revival is always costly. Yet, the glory of the Acts revival, and every true move of God, is that the gospel is spread by the least-likely people to the darkest places of the world. If you read Acts carefully, you will see that the revival on the day of Pentecost affected people gathered in Jerusalem from all over the world. This was purposeful. God poured out his Spirit on thousands of people from a vast array of nations so that they could spread the gospel to their homelands. The first evangelists to take the revival outside of Jerusalem were not the apostles, but ordinary people from the nations of the world.

TWEET: @Jacob McAuley

Evangelism can be organized, Revival cannot. - Leonard Ravenhill

WHAT REVIVAL LOOKS LIKE

The apostles were filled with the Spirit, revived, and became fiery leaders in Jerusalem. Thousands were saved on the day of Pentecost. Then what? What happens as God begins to pour out His Spirit on the church? What should happen? Is there a biblical pattern for what to expect? I believe so. Let's take a closer look at Acts 2:41-47:

> "So those who received his word were baptized, and there were added that day three thousand souls. And they devoted themselves to the apostles teaching and the breaking of bread and the prayers. And awe came upon every soul, and many wonders and signs were being done through the apostles. And all who believed were together and had all things in common. And they were selling their possessions and belongings and distributing the proceeds to all, as any had need. And day by day, attending the temple together and breaking bread in their homes, they received their food with glad and generous hearts, praising God and having favor with all the people. And the Lord added to their number day by day those who were being saved."

Marks of Revival from Acts 2:

- Public preaching

- Baptisms

- Devotion to the Word

- Lord's Supper

- Prayer

- Awe of God

- Miracles

- Unity

- Sacrificial giving

- Meeting needs

- Daily fellowship

- Corporate worship

- Meals in homes

- Thankfulness

- Praise of God

- Favor and salvations

The marks of revival in Acts 2 show two prime areas of transformation, one inside the church and one outside. The more revival heats up, the move of God within the church begins to spill outside the church. Those inside the church begin to increase in devotion to the Word, enjoying the Lord's Supper, prayer, unity, serving, daily fellowship, awe in worship, experiencing miracles, thankfulness, salvations, and baptisms. All these aspects of the normal Christian life are increased in power, meaning, and significance. The church begins to wake up and experience God at work in her midst. As God revives His people, He begins to work in extraordinary ways within the church family. People love, pray, fellowship, give, sacrifice, and grow as never before! As this outpouring reaches a boiling point, the Holy Spirit begins to overflow His blessings out to the world at large.

On the day of Pentecost, this happened almost immediately. The Holy Spirit was poured out resulting in dramatic sounds, winds, fire, and tongues. Yet this was not for the enjoyment of the people of God alone, but was immediately joined by the miraculous drawing of thousands of people to the steps of the upper room to allow God's move to spread to the masses. Isn't it amazing that the revival God is planning to send to our churches is actually a revival meant for the masses of lost and dying people in our cities and nations? In my short experience in the prayer movement, I have seen God's response to the prayers of His people—launching movements that are carried outside the walls of the building to engage the city by meeting physical, emotional, relational, spiritual, and financial needs.

I love the book of Acts because it shows that God's work is not meant for buildings, but must go to our streets and neighborhoods. Pentecost took the church public on day one. Frankly, there was no time to strategize about the best way to reach the city. God empowered Peter and the other apostles to preach Jesus and see the Holy Spirit do miracles in confirmation of the Word. In Acts, we also see the spread of the gospel from Jerusalem to other cities, regions, and nations. We see the Holy Spirit begin to empower non-apostolic leaders to be used powerfully in ministry in Jerusalem and around the world. In fact, the church in Antioch, the first missionary sending church, was established by ordinary believers who were more than likely saved at Pentecost or influenced by those who were. Acts is a beautiful picture of what God is doing today. He is moving the church outside its walls, and giving the ministry to the entire body of Christ, regardless of title, age, maturity, or status. Jesus wants to empower all His people to do all the ministry!

✈TWEET: @DavidSliker

Revival is both a small "preview" of the Second Coming, as well as a catalyst to hasten the day (Acts 3:19-21); let us contend unceasingly!

The mission field is enormous and it will require all of us to do all of the work. It's a joyous task to be used of the Holy Spirit in ministry. There is almost nothing I know that compares with it. Over the years, I have surveyed church members as to the specific times they felt closest to Jesus. I was hoping they might tell me it was when I was preaching or maybe during worship. Surprisingly, virtually everyone said they felt closest to God when they were knee-deep in active ministry. We were made to pray and we were made to minister, both inside and outside the church.

The book of Acts helps us see that revival is not an event as much as it is a lifestyle. What happened on the day of Pentecost was indeed the catalyst, but true revival was found in the daily passions and practices of these earliest revivalists. We can't live in the upper room! Many times in church history we've seen revivals launched only to die out far too quickly. Yet, in some amazing way, you and I are products of the first New Testament revival at Pentecost. This is the same glorious work that was promised by Jesus in Acts 1:8:

> "But you will receive power when the Holy Spirit has come
> upon you, and you will be my witnesses in Jerusalem and in
> all Judea and Samaria, and to the end of the earth."

We are the fruit of this promise. The Holy Spirit's work that began at Pentecost has continued uninterrupted on the earth, and has now reached our day and our community in the United States, almost two thousand years later. Amazing! This excites me and gives me great hope. The fires of revival which began at Pentecost have never left the earth. The original flames have burned brightly on occasions, while maintaining only a small flicker much of the time. Often the fires of revival were carried in the hearts of obscure or unknown believers. God has always had a revived people on the earth. And now, by God's sovereign hand, the same work of the Spirit's power is available to us today, right now. This is so encouraging!

I don't want to leave this earth without seeing my beloved city of Austin turned right-side up, to become the live worship capital of the world. That's part of what I believe is God's destiny for her. As well as being a leadership city, called to create legislation through government, Austin is also intended to raise up spiritual leaders who shape history. We are not called merely to be a city that educates more than a hundred thousand college students, but we are called to reach them, disciple them in Christ, and send them out to the nations of the earth. Think about what you see in your city and how its natural DNA is created to be a spiritual reality spreading revival across the city and the earth. A great resource to aid you in working through this process is *Taking Our Cities For God* by John Dawson.

I believe God is going to establish 24/7 houses of prayer and worship throughout the greater Austin area. People will be able to go day or night, any day of the year, north, south, east, or west, and experience the presence of God there. In addition to having 24/7 prayer and worship, these houses of prayer will be hubs for 24/7 outreach serving the needs of the community. Can you imagine the impact of literally dozens of 24/7 houses of prayer that reach out to the community with overflowing love, day and night? This is the essence of revival. This is what I dream of seeing not only in Austin, but in your city, too, and in all the cities of the world. Our First Commandment passion to love God will fuel Second Commandment compassion and practical expressions of love. What a beautiful picture of the revived church!

As the church is revived, the gospel will invade the darkest parts of the city, which have been previously untouched by the church. In Austin, those locations will include 6th Street, which has been largely set apart for live music, drinking, and partying. I believe precursors of revival are seen when the church begins to arise and share Jesus' love with those in the darkest areas of the city. We must not wait until revival hits to take the gospel to the most oppressed parts of our city. We must go to these sections not in protest, but with deep love and compassion for those trapped in darkness.

In 2009 we experienced two dramatic examples that God is awakening His people to pray and act in love in areas normally forsaken by Christians. Following a special season and empowerment to pray, Christians led by Joe

Elliott of the Catalyst Teen Center, began to go Austin's notorious 6th Street, the city's party capital, to pray for people who asked for it or were open to prayer. We sought to bring more visibility to our mission by wearing the most garish, bright orange tee-shirts you've ever seen, with the words "Prayer Team" on the front. Every month for the past five years, Christians from various churches have joined for united prayer, and then walked the streets in a setting most clearly resembling the party atmosphere you would see at New Orleans' infamous Mardi Gras—except it occurs nightly in our city.

It's hard to explain what God has done through this ministry, especially in us. We have sown seeds among the lost, seen several come to know Christ, fed the homeless, encouraged the wayward believer, and prayed for countless people. Until we began going to pray, walk, and minister on 6th Street, we had no idea that the first Protestant church in Austin began there in the 1830s, with five people. Then it hit us: we were once again claiming ground that the church had first occupied, before it was given over to the enemy to steal, kill, and destroy. We are a part of the new, awakened army of love sent to reclaim ground sacred to the work of the Lord, and the destiny of the city. Instead of commonly expected judgment, God has allowed us to share His healing and restoring love with some of even the most hardened hearts. We are not on 6th Street to preach or condemn; our mission is one of prayer, love, and service. We await the day when the city-church will work together to establish a live worship, prayer, and ministry center right in the heart of the bar district there. We view this not as a possibility but as a God-secured destiny.

The second dramatic prayer and ministry event in some of the darkest corners of our city was forged by a pro-life group called Central Texas Coalition for Life, founded and led primarily by young Catholic believers. Twice a year Coalition for Life has organized Forty Days for Life events, where area Christians adopt an hour or more a week to stand in front of the four Austin abortion clinics and pray peacefully for an end to abortion. Other trained volunteers go as "sidewalk counselors," speaking lovingly to those going into the clinic, and offering compassionate and free alternatives. In the past five years, 187 babies have been rescued as a result. Imagine the pain and horror that so many babies, women, fathers, and families have been spared all because Christians believe that the best places to pray and love are the darkest areas of the city. Once again, we have seen that "mercy triumphs over judgment" (James 2:13).

Other examples in Austin reveal that God is indeed up to something new. A special outpouring of the Spirit in 2008 began calling believers to pray as never before. The church had been praying in the preceding years, but a new, unified wind of the Spirit began calling us to pray for our city in a new way. When God ignites His people to pray, it's because He surely plans to launch them into new forms of ministry. As we began praying as a church in new, unprecedented ways, God began launching new ministries.

Some began feeding the homeless regularly, which they still do all these years later. Others began reaching out to Austin Community College through a student organization our church formed called Love In Transit (LIT). It continues to be the only Christian presence reaching out to over fifty thousand students. Now, other churches have joined the effort. The yearly pastor's prayer gathering, which normally had around seventy pastors in attendance, has more than doubled in size. When a hundred and fifty pastors from across various denominations gather for two days of prayer together, God is on the move!

🐦TWEET: *@ScottyWardSmith*

When God manifests himself w/ such glorious power in a work of revival, he appears especially determined 2 put honor upon his Son. - J Edwards

The book of Acts is about missions—how the Holy Spirit fell on the day of Pentecost and immediately began reaching the nations with salvation. It's about these new believers returning home with the fire of God in their hearts, spreading it to their families and neighbors, and establishing new churches wherever they went. The book of Acts demonstrates what happens when a church is filled with the reviving work of the Holy Spirit. It's not a perfect scene. For sure, persecution, division, rivalry, and selfishness still arise, but the spreading of the Word and the sacrificing of God's people triumph over the lesser rivals. God moved the gospel from an upper room in Jerusalem and spread the truth all the way to Rome and beyond. He desires to do the same today. He longs to pour out His Spirit and move you from the place of prayer to the nations of the earth, or the mission field right in your own backyard.

Remember, we are not waiting for revival to come some day. We are contending for it right here, right now. You don't have to wait for your pastor, church, or denomination to experience revival. You can experience God-sent revival all by yourself. Set your heart to humble yourself, pray, seek God's face, and turn from your wicked ways. Ask God to pour out the Holy Spirit on you. Remember, He loves to answer that prayer (Luke 11:13). As He begins to revive you, you will begin to see everything differently. You will find God filling your heart with an ever-increasing passion for Him and a contagious compassion for others. You will begin to see all of life as your ministry. Like John Wesley you will say, "The world is my parish!"

I believe most Christians hold an incorrect view of missions. I understand why: we've been taught that missions is crossing a culture to bring Jesus to a lesser-reached group or community. Since most of us live and will probably die in the United States, we do not see ourselves as missionaries. They are those who wear funny clothes and periodically show up at church with a random slide show and a few newsletters. Most believers are sure they are not missionaries. But that's because we have not been taught correctly. The final frontier will be reached by ordinary believers who live like missionaries to reach anyone and everyone they meet.

Let's take the traditional definition of the word "missionary" and tweak it a bit. Missions involves a believer taking Jesus to a different culture that is less evangelized. Now, we as Christians are called foreigners and aliens on this earth (1 Pet. 2:11), so we qualify as being from a different culture than everyone who is unsaved. That includes Americans that look just like us. And if they are unsaved, then they qualify as less evangelized than we. Do you get the picture? We are all missionaries, ordained by God to reach people in our neighborhoods, work places, families, and cities.

Recently, while reading a book called *The Next Christians* by Gabe Lyons, I came across a very helpful chart that noted what he called the "Seven Areas of Influence." These are the arts, media, education, social, political, business, and church spheres. That's when it hit me: we've been training and sending missionaries out to un-evangelized countries for years, but we have not been raising up the rank-and-file members of our churches and commissioning them as missionaries to these seven areas of influence. We have thousands of saved believers who think they are second-rate Christians because they are not in "full-time ministry," when all along they are the ones who are supposed to be trained, commissioned, and sent out as missionaries, or change agents, to these seven areas of influence here at home.

God wants to revive you in order to send you out to reach the people in the world that He loves who are resisting Him. He wants to use your time, your job, your personality, your gifts, your money, your body, and yes, even your voice, to proclaim Jesus to individuals. Normally speaking, missions involves a one-to-one relationship rather than one overwhelming evangelistic event. People are saved, changed, and touched because someone took an interest in them and shared Jesus with them personally. I am deeply struck by these words in Romans 10:14-15:

> "How then will they call on him in whom they have not believed? And how are they to believe in Him of whom they have never heard? And how are they to hear without

someone preaching? And how are they to preach unless they are sent? As it is written, 'How beautiful are the feet of those who preach the good news!'"

Do you see the chain of events? Someone with beautiful feet was sent to preach the gospel to you. You heard the good news and, because you heard, you believed. Now, the chain continues. Because you believed, you are now commissioned to go and share the good news with those who are still lost. The point is clear: lost people must believe in order to be saved. And for that to occur, saved people must preach. For that to happen, believers must realize they are commissioned by God to go. Simply put, Jesus will not save people apart from our verbal witness of Christ. God has no Plan B: you are the method He uses to change the world!

What an exciting day in which to live, when the world is ripe for real solutions from real people like us. Don't wait until you are perfect. If you do, you won't ever go! Go tell people that only God is perfect, and that He sent you because He loves them. Tell them you struggle like they do, but you have met the one whose love has revolutionized your world with true hope. Tell them you've been sent with a message that they must hear: it's too good and too important not to be told. As you go, make much of Jesus (that's humility), pray (that shows you know it's impossible to make a difference without God), seek God (knowing He's your joy whether they accept or reject your message), and turn from your wicked ways (so Satan won't sidetrack you from being an agent of change).

Is it starting to make sense? Revival does not happen when the church has long meetings so we can see cool things happen. At the heart of revival is a Father who "so loves the world that He sent His only Son so that whoever believes in Him will not perish, but have everlasting life" (John 3:16). Revival awakens the church to who Jesus died to make us—lovers of God and lovers of others. We cannot wait for a someday revival. We must plead with God to revive our hearts today so we can be mobilized to reach every man, woman, and child with the life-changing message of Jesus Christ.

The church must wake up. Time is short. We must repent of being involved in civilian affairs. No more excuses. God has given everything we need for life and godliness. We have been created for such a time as this. This is your one chance to make an eternal, heaven-or-hell difference on planet earth. Do not miss the day of your calling. Begin today. Start praying now. Walk in response to your prayers. Share Jesus with someone. Pray with a hurting friend. Share the hope you have inside. Revival must begin now, and it must be shared with all who will listen. God is worthy. Revival will be worth any sacrifice you make.

Revival Cry

SMALL GROUP QUESTIONS

1. Do you have a hope or a dream of God sending revival? Explain.

2. Restate 2 Chronicles 7:14 in your own words. Why is the passage vital to us experiencing revival?

3. What strikes you most in Acts 2:1-14? Why? Do you believe God can revive us today?

4. What occurred in the Jerusalem church after Pentecost (Acts 2:42-47)? Are you involved in any of these things?

5. Why do you think it's been hundreds of years since America experienced a widespread revival?

6. Are you willing to give your life contending for revival? Explain.

7. When people begin to pray God always launches them into ministry in the darkest areas. How have you seen this to be true?

8. What characteristics of your city do you see that God wants to use for His glory?

9. How would your life, family, and job change if you approached them as a missionary?

10. Explain "revival cry" in your own words.

REVIVAL CRY ACTION ITEM

Find someone from a younger generation and go through this book with them.

CHAPTER 8

THE MOST IMPORTANT LESSONS FROM THE FIRST GREAT AWAKENING

I thought I was finished writing *Revival Cry* when, on a prayer walk, I felt God tell me to add three new chapters—one on the First Great Awakening, another on the Second Great Awakening, and finally another on the coming Third Great Awakening. The goal is to learn lessons from past events that were so powerfully widespread they earned the distinctive title "Great Awakenings." We are in need of such an awakening today more than ever! It is what believers throughout the earth are crying out for day and night. Can you imagine how pleased Father God must be that His children across racial, socio-economic, and denominational backgrounds are contending 24/7 for a worldwide Third Great Awakening? God promises in Luke 18:7-8:

> "And will not God give justice to his elect, who cry out to him night and day? Will he delay long over them? I tell you, he will give justice to them speedily."

Between 1720 and 1760, parts of Europe and much of America experienced what has now been called the First Great Awakening. This historic move of God not only shaped the very fabric of the growing republic in America, but is still molding the global prayer movement. Even today, modern believers look back to the 1720s to gain inspiration to persevere in 24/7 prayer that will erupt in a new missions movement.

Let us consider four main characters from three different countries in the First Great Awakening: Count Zinzendorf from Germany, George Whitefield and John Wesley from England, and Jonathan Edwards from America. Zinzendorf, an Austrian noble born in 1700, led a small community of radicals known as the Moravians into what he called "heart religion." This community experienced transforming revival that resulted in a hundred-year prayer meeting, and an unparalleled missions movement throughout the earth. Whitefield and Wesley, contemporaries at Oxford in England in 1729, both played key roles in the spread of the fires of revival in England and America. Jonathan Edwards, who became a pastor in Northampton, Massachusetts in 1729, was a key figure in the awakenings that hit America. These men will help us understand seven key lessons that are essential for the American church and the global body of Christ to experience a Third Great Awakening.

LESSON ONE: Revival Flows From Community

As we see in Acts, revival is birthed in the community of God known as the church. Jesus promised in Matthew 16:18, "I will build my church, and the gates of hell shall not prevail against it." Many today have given up on the church—but God hasn't. We are His method of changing the world. In his classic book *Power Through Prayer*, E.M. Bounds says, "Men are looking for better methods, but God is looking for better men."[9] The great need today is not better methods, strategies, or models of church—if these could change the world we would have seen revival long ago. We need God's church brought back to the power experienced by Zinzendorf, Wesley, Whitefield, and Edwards. Mighty outpourings of the Holy Spirit resulted in fiery Christians full of love who burned with zeal for the lost and took Jesus' message all over the world. Today, as then, revival flows out of Christ's community.

Zinzendorf began one of the first known modern missional communities in Herrnhut, Germany in 1722. By 1727 this struggling community was deeply divided, with much backbiting and deep division. Zinzendorf began calling the community to a basic Christian covenant of love and prayer. God began to pour out His Spirit in various meetings that affected children and adults alike, resulting in prayer meetings and praise services that sometimes lasted all night. This climaxed in a community communion service that has been called the Moravian Pentecost.

God poured out His Spirit in such a mighty way that this group was transformed to radically embody the three characteristics that define any truly revived community: love, prayer, and missions. The point is clear; no matter what state your church or expression of the body of Christ is in, God can and will revive His people. Jesus died to enable His people to live with burning, passionate love for Him and others. This is the right and result of the new birth. And when God does this in a community, their joy and influence is multiplied.

Whitefield and Wesley formed a "holy club" at Oxford that took seriously the pursuit of moral living. The irony was that neither of these young men was born-again at the time. Whitefield was the first to experience salvation through grace. Wesley, on the other hand, became a pastor and even came to America on a mission trip before he was saved. On the boat ride home from both a failed romance and a failed mission in the United States, Wesley saw in the Moravians a kind of real Christianity he had previously not known. Providentially Wesley's heart was later "strangely warmed"—his term for being saved—at a Moravian meeting in England.

Once again, the community of God was pivotal in birthing another fiery revivalist who would later shake not only America, but much of the earth with a new brand of "heart religion." Wesley would later be credited not only with founding the Methodist church, but with fathering the Holiness and Pentecostal churches worldwide. Whitefield's unique contribution was his commitment to an interdenominational approach in partnering with all the lovers of Jesus in England and America. This is key because, as the great theologian of revival Dr. Edwin Orr says, "Every great awakening has been interdenominational." Edwards took over the Northampton church from his grandfather in 1729, and said it was like preaching to "dry bones."

The congregation—like most on earth today—was desperately in need of revival. Edwards said the town experienced a "degenerate time" with "dullness of religion." In 1734 two well-known young people died. This deeply shook the community. Edwards preached strong messages calling the people back to God, and in December of 1734, six young people were converted. One young lady with a well-known reputation was dramatically changed by God's power. In the next six months, three hundred of the town's eleven hundred residents were radically saved—a quarter of the population.[10] Revival had begun in a small church in a small community—but that was just the beginning of what God had in mind!

LESSON TWO: Revival Follows Prayer

Zinzendorf learned early the importance of prayer in the community of God's people. At just sixteen he established seven prayer societies at his boarding school. This practice continued as he forged the community at Herrnhut, where he was grieved by the deep carnality and petty divisions among the people there. He knew that fresh outpourings of the Spirit follow the cries of God's people. What happened at Herrnhut is so earth-shattering that Christians still make the pilgrimage to the small German town today, seeking to learn the secrets of the Holy Spirit's outpouring that resulted in a hundred-year prayer meeting and the most radical missions movement since the book of Acts. What did they have that we don't, that would enable this small community of a few hundred people to pray night and day for a century, sending out hundreds of missionaries—some who would gladly sell themselves into slavery to reach other slaves?

The answer: their God was real, their mission was essential, and their prayers were a way of life. Prayer not only launched the Moravians into revival, but also helped sustain it. In 1727, twenty-four men and twenty-four women committed, as a lifestyle, to adopt one hour of prayer each day to ensure the "watch of the Lord" continued round the clock. Revival historian David Smithers says of Zinzendorf: "The best antidote for a powerless Church is the influence of a praying man. The influence of Count Zinzendorf's prayer-life did not stop with one small community. It ultimately went on to influence the whole world."[11]

Through their missionary endeavors, these Moravians established life-giving communities all over the world. Wesley and Whitefield both were deeply changed by the Moravian "Love Feasts," or community meals, that often resulted in the Spirit's dramatic outpourings such that they would pray all night. Whitefield wrote in his journal:

> "Sometimes whole nights were spent in prayer. Often have we been filled as with new wine. And often have we seen them overwhelmed with the Divine presence and crying out, 'Will God indeed dwell with men upon earth! How dreadful is this place! This is none other than the house of God and the gates of Heaven."[12]

On Sunday Jan. 7, 1739 George Whitefield recorded that another "love feast" took place where the brothers gathered, shared a meal together and then prayed through the night. "There was a great pouring out of the Spirit amongst the brethren," he noted.[13] Wesley reflected after his first visit to Herrnhut, "When will this kind of Christianity fill the earth?" The DNA of community and prayer that the Moravians embraced in Herrnhut had been exported around the world and was now impacting a new generation of revivalists in Wesley and Whitefield. These men would be the key agents to see revival burst forth both in England and America.

Edwards would learn the power and centrality of prayer both before the awakening in America and after it died out. As the church in Northampton struggled to impact the "degenerate" township, a small band of prayer warriors cried out for God to move. "Soon the awakening spread throughout the entire thirteen colonies. It was the first national experience and Jonathan Edwards would be called the 'Great Awakener'," notes historian Paul Dienstberger.[14] We know that Edwards understood that prayer was the source of the First Great Awakening because as the fires of revival that had burned throughout the colonies began to die out, he wrote a book called *A Humble Attempt To Promote Prayer For Revival*, calling the church in America to united prayer every week for revival.

"Edwards wrote this book in 1746 after seeing two remarkable movements of the Spirit of God, one during 1734-35 and the other in 1740-42," noted revival historian Tony Cauchi. "He was convinced that Christian prayers for revival released the power of God's Spirit and resulted in

converts and would bring worldwide revival."[15] Edwards would die twelve
years later, in 1758, while still wholeheartedly contending for the next move
of God. He would not see it from earth, but this historic call to united
prayer would pave the way for the upcoming Second Great Awakening.

LESSON THREE: Revival Explodes From Spirit-Anointed Preaching

Zinzendorf's zeal for Christ and preaching Christ saturated all he did,
every word he wrote, and any sermon he preached. He cried, "Preach the
gospel, be forgotten and die"—strong words from a man of great wealth
who chose rather to invest his life and money in building a community to
change the world. His stated life purpose was, "I have one passion; it is
Christ, and Christ alone." For Zinzendorf the preaching of the gospel was
to preach Christ. He said Paul did not make anything known among the
heathen except Jesus.[16] *The Moravian Church Miscellany* states that Zinzendorf
taught his followers the key to anointed preaching:

> "Our method to proclaim salvation is this: to point out to
> every heart the loving Lamb (das herzliche Lamm) which
> died for us, and although he was the Son of God, offered
> himself for our sins—as his God, his Mediator between God
> and man, his preacher of the law, his Confessor, his
> Comforter, his Saviour, his throne of grace, his example, his
> brother, in short his all and in all, by the preaching of his
> blood, and of his love unto death, even the death on the
> cross; never, either in the discourse or in argument, to
> digress even for a quarter of an hour from the loving Lamb;
> to name no virtue, except in Him and from Him and on His
> account; to preach no commandment except faith in him; no
> other justification but that he atoned for us; no other
> sanctification but the privilege to sin no more; no other
> happiness, but to be around him, to think of him and do his
> pleasure; no other self-denial, but to be deprived of him and
> his blessings; no other calamity, but to displease him; no
> other life, but in him."[17]

Whitefield is known as the greatest revival preacher in history, speaking
to larger audiences than any man up to that point. Today our preaching is
pragmatic and user-friendly. The preaching of the First Great Awakening
was dynamic and heart-felt, and could as easily move an audience to tears or
to fall down in repentance. Whitefield was a dramatic preacher with a voice
like no other—one that could carry up to a mile and be heard by more than
twenty thousand people without the aid of a microphone. This is
astounding in itself, but even more remarkable was the powerful anointing
that compelled thousands to come hear him preach wherever he went. He

was also an innovator. When many denominational churches closed their doors to his evangelical preaching, he responded by taking his preaching outdoors to the masses. He learned this from fellow preachers in Wales, but he made outdoor preaching acceptable in England and America. Whitefield urged and facilitated the outdoor preaching of John and Charles Wesley.

Cauchi noted in The First Great Awakening in America: "In late 1735 the New England revival had begun to decline. But Whitefield's arrival heralded the second wave of blessing. He took it to heights it had never before attained, inspiring a host of others to engage in revival work...thousands flocked to hear him...in just one six-week tour at this time he preached over one hundred and seventy-five sermons to tens of thousands of people, leaving the region in a spiritual upheaval."[18] The awakening in America reached its pinnacle with Whitefield's preaching. "The crowd in the Boston Commons was estimated at 23,000 people...more than the population of Boston," says Dienstberger, "80% of the American people heard Whitefield preach at least one sermon."[19]

The same unprecedented results followed Whitefield's preaching in England. Consider these astounding journal entries from 1739:

Wednesday, May 2. Preached this evening to above 10,000 at Kennington Common...

Saturday, May 5. Preached yesterday and today as usual at Kennington Common, to about twenty thousand hearers, who were very much affected

Sunday, May 6. Preached this morning in Moorfields to about twenty thousand people...much affected. Went to public worship morning and evening, and at six preached at Kennington. Such a sight I never saw before. I believe there was no less than fifty thousand people, and near four score coaches, besides the great numbers of horses. God gave me great enlargement of heart. I continued my discourse for an hour and a half, and when I returned home I was filled with such love, peace and joy that I cannot express it.

*Tuesday, May 8...*before I set out from town it rained very hard...To my great surprise, when I came to the Common I saw above twenty thousand people. All the while...the sun shone upon us; and I trust the Sun of Righteousness arose on some with healing in his wings.

Thursday, May 10. Preached at Kennington, but it rained most of the day. There were not above ten thousand people and thirty coaches. However, God was pleased so visible to interpose in causing the weather to clear up and the sun to shine out just as I began, that I could not avoid taking notice of it in my discourse.[20]

Edwards is best known for preaching powerful and daunting messages which launched the revival in Northampton and throughout the New England area, eventually spreading like wildfire throughout the colonies. Edwards was an anointed preacher, but very different in style from his friend Whitefield. Edwards was a staid preacher who read deliberately from his manuscript, yet no preacher I've read about in the First Great Awakening had more dramatic results. People were overwhelmingly stricken with tears, or rendered unable to move. Some would be slain to the ground by God's convicting power. The most dramatic of Edwards' revival launching sermons is "Sinners In the Hands of An Angry God." First preached at his church without dramatic effects, it later launched widespread revival in area churches. Though it is the best known of Edwards' sermons, it is by no means typical. Edwards is known as the greatest theological mind in American history. He studied and prayed for many hours daily, preaching on a wide array of topics including love, joy, and faith, all rooted in the sovereignty of God.

Zinzendorf preached simply Christ. Whitefield was extemporaneous, dramatic, and public, but powerfully anointed. Edward's preaching was studied and deliberate, yet equally powerful. The point is not the style or the method. The goal is anointed preaching. Preachers must once again find God in secret, as these men did, and proclaim a fiery message from Him in the pulpit. A. W. Tozer says that today we have promoters and politicians in the pulpit, when we need prophets who have heard from God and enter the pulpit with a holy message. Unfortunately the current trend in preaching is toward gaining followers rather than igniting revivalists. May a new generation of prophetic preachers arise in America and around the world!

LESSON FOUR: Revival Results in Conversions

This seems like the most obvious of the lessons, but unless folks are being dramatically converted inside and outside the church, then revival is not taking place. I use the word "conversion" two-fold. First, indicating the saving of the lost. Second, describing the reviving of the lukewarm. The trend in the church, both past and present, is toward lukewarmness. Left to ourselves, we drift toward half-heartedness. The church in America, both at our founding and in our present—and most days in between—has been primarily characterized by those who have lost our "first love." In his book *The History of Redemption*, Edwards says "though there be a more constant influence of God's Spirit always, in some degree, attending His ordinances;

yet the way in which the greatest things have been done towards carrying on this work, always has been by remarkable effusions of the Spirit at special seasons of mercy.' "

The Moravians are the epitome of a revived community. Consider these heart-warming accounts from 1727 of the community awakenings among the Moravians, from revivalist archives:

> "On the Lord's day, the 10th of August, the minister Rothe was seized, in the midst of the assembly, with an unusual impulse. He threw himself upon his knees before God, and the whole assembly prostrated themselves with him under the same emotions. An uninterrupted course of singing and prayer, weeping and supplication, continued till midnight. All hearts were united in love."

> "On Wednesday, 13th August, the Holy Spirit was poured out on whole assembly. During the communion service, loud weeping drowned out the singing. An electric anointing flowed through all those present with inexpressible joy and love as they all shared the bread and wine, knowing they were baptized into one Spirit. The scene was so moving that the pastor could hardly tell what he saw or heard."

> "A few days after the 13th of August, a remarkable revival took place among the children at Herrnhut and Bertholdsdorf. On the 18th of August, all the children at the boarding school were seized with an extraordinary impulse of the Spirit, and spent the whole night in prayer. From this time, a constant work of God was going on in the minds of the children, in both places. No words can express the powerful operation of the Holy Spirit upon these children, whose lives were so transformed."[21]

What is most striking is that the revival affected adults and children alike; may God do the same in our communities today!

As previously noted, Edwards saw the dramatic conversion of notoriously sinful teens from the community. This resulted in a powerful move of God, and the saving of a quarter of the population of Northampton. Imagine one in four in your city being saved. In the greater Austin area, which includes 1.7 million people, that would be 425,000 conversions. God can do it again!

Historians estimate that a further twenty thousand were converted through Whitefield's numerous visits to America from 1730 onwards. A hundred and fifty new Congregational churches were established in twenty years. The Baptists increased from nine churches to four hundred, with a total membership of thirty thousand. Other denominations had similar growth. Nine colleges were established as a result of the First Great Awakening. "Many colleges made their entrance requirement a salvation experience in Jesus Christ and had a stated purpose to propagate the gospel," says Paul Dienstberger.[22]

LESSON FIVE: Revival Is Perpetuated Through Unified Fellowships

Divided churches are carnal churches that remain unrevived. One sign of a revived church is that more of the members come together for the glory and honor of Jesus alone. This doesn't mean there will be no opposition. That would be an extremely naive view. Yet, as God revives His church, His people rally around the goals of loving God and spreading His love to others worldwide. This is the sign of unity. Whether we like each other's personalities or we agree politically is not the issue. A unified church is on mission with God to see the world turned right-side up in zealous love for Him and others. This drives the unified and revived church.

Zinzendorf was initially inspired to pray for a fresh outpouring of the Spirit because his local church was so petty in its divisions, backbiting, and gossip. He drew up a community contract and asked all the members to sign an agreement toward unity. This was good, but it was not the cause of the transformation. Change occurred as the body was broken over its sin and began to turn to God in repentance and prayer for transformation. Prayer became the hallmark of a unified church. Today, God is unifying His church by calling us to united prayer. All of our differences fade as we join together to "humble ourselves under God's mighty hand" in prayer. This lifestyle is what forges ongoing unity for any and every community. In Acts, the scattered disciples joined together for ten days of round-the-clock prayer leading to unity and a mighty outpouring of the Holy Spirit. "All these with one accord were devoting themselves to prayer," says Acts 1:14. May God do this simple and transforming work of unity and prayer in our churches and in our cities.

Wesley and Whitefield experienced so much opposition from the existing church that they were forced outside its doors to preach in the highways and byways. Wesley's journal shows the powerful opposition he faced both in the established churches and outside in the streets:

> ***Sunday, A.M., May 5*** Preached in St. Anne's. Was asked not to come back anymore.

> ***Sunday, P.M., May 5*** Preached in St. John's. Deacons said "Get out and stay out."

Sunday, A.M., May 12 Preached in St. Jude's. Can't go back there, either.

Sunday, A.M., May 19 Preached in St. Somebody Else's. Deacons called special meeting and said I couldn't return.

Sunday, P.M., May 19 Preached on street. Kicked off street.

Sunday, A.M., May 26 Preached in meadow. Chased out of a meadow as bull was turned loose during service.

Sunday, A.M., June 2 Preached out at the edge of town. Kicked off the highway.

Sunday, P.M., June 2 Afternoon, preached in a pasture. Ten thousand people came out to hear me.[23]

Edwards notes that he began his ministry preaching to dead "dry bones." God began to revive the church and they saw great unity and community transformation. Yet, as we tend to do, the church later fell back to its old ways and resented Edward's leadership toward a more pure and truly unified church. In the one of the most shocking moves in church history, the great revivalist of the First Great Awakening was fired from his church. "June 22 is the anniversary of Jonathan Edwards' dismissal from his pastorate in 1750," notes Fred Sanders. "The great awakening had gone through his town a few years before, but once it was over, plenty of people wanted to go back to sleep. Edwards had tried to raise the standards for church membership and communion in his town, and discovered that his town didn't really intend to act like revival had ever happened."[24]

The moral to these stories: revival must be an ongoing occurrence. We cannot rely on what God has done in the past to carry us forward. Without a revived heart, moment by moment, we are susceptible to the schemes of the enemy causing us to be drawn away by our own evil desires. Revival is about forging unity around God and His goals—not around our preferences or desires. If we are not careful, the most religious among us can find ourselves being used by the enemy, yelling, "Crucify Him!"

LESSON SIX: Revival Results In Missions

Zinzendorf's spiritual DNA was forged as a child in boarding schools as he and his friends formed secret Christian societies. Their stated goal was to spread the gospel around the world. "In 1722, in his early twenties, he opened up his estate in Saxony to provide sanctuary for religious refugees fleeing persecution," says historian Steve Addison. "They built a village, Herrnhut meaning "the Lord's watch".[25] In January of 1728 they held their first missionary meeting. On October 8, 1732 a Dutch ship left the Copenhagen harbor bound for the Danish West Indies. "On board were the two first Moravian missionaries; John Leonard Dober, a potter, and David Nitschman, a carpenter," noted revival historian David Smithers. "Both were skilled speakers and ready to sell themselves into slavery to reach the slaves of the West Indies. As the ship slipped away, they lifted up a cry that would one day become the rallying call for all Moravian missionaries, 'May the Lamb that was slain receive the reward of His suffering.' The Moravian's passion for souls was surpassed only by their passion for the Lamb of God, Jesus Christ." In the next twenty-five years the Moravians sent out hundreds of missionaries from this small community. They established more than two hundred mission stations before William Carey—now known as the father of modern missions—was even born.[26]

The First Great Awakening was formed and forged through missions. Wesley and Whitefield made many trips from their motherland in England to America, adding fresh fire to the embers of revival and launching a new season of spiritual blessing. Whitefield followed Wesley's advice to go to America. He sailed in 1737, aged twenty-three, and ministered in America for one year. The results were staggering. The Great Awakening saw fifty thousand souls saved out of a quarter of a million people in New England. The middle states experienced similar results, with over one hundred towns being dramatically changed. Hundreds of new churches were planted. Much of this occurred during Whitefield's seven extended trips to American between 1737 and 1770.[27] In addition, Whitfield traveled to other parts of the world to preach: revival produces missionaries!

Edward's influence over the growing missionary movement would come about in a most unexpected way. Edwards would influence missions by telling the story of David Brainerd—a young man kicked out of Yale Divinity School for his comment about the unregenerate nature of a teacher. Brainerd's expulsion from college closed every door of ministry to him except becoming a missionary to the American Indians. Although he lived only to the age of twenty-nine, Brainerd's influence on missions is incalculable. The dramatic, heart-wrenching, exhilarating diary he kept while ministering to the Indians may never have influenced the Christian world had he not come to live with the Edwards family just prior to his death.

Brainerd was desperately sick with consumption and, in a short time, died of tuberculosis. Edwards's seventeen-year-old daughter, Jerusha, who is said to have fallen in love with Brainerd, also later died of tuberculosis after nursing him. Edwards felt Brainerd's story and diary must be shared with the world. He put off other important writing assignments to write *An Account of the Life of the Late Reverend Mr. David Brainerd*. According to contemporary preacher John Piper, "As a result of the immense impact of Brainerd's devotion on Jonathan Edwards, Edwards wrote in the next two years the *Life of Brainerd*, which has been reprinted more often than any of his other books. And through this Life the impact of Brainerd on the church has been incalculable, because beyond all the famous missionaries who tell us that they have been sustained and inspired by Brainerd's Life how many countless other unknown faithful servants must there be who found strength to press on from Brainerd's testimony!"[28]

Edwards not only inspired believers to become missionaries through his writings but, like Brainerd, was himself unexpectedly called to be missionary to the American Indians. "The last chapter" of Edwards' life and ministry, according to Professor Edward Panosian, was "the fruitful harvest at Stockbridge, sixty miles away. Here, Edwards was called to be a pastor to a small flock and missionary to the Housatunnock Indians. Twelve white families and 250 Indian families made up the population. Not well-fitted for such a role, yet isolated still farther from the bustle of the world, he was given now of God the opportunity to reap with his pen the harvest of decades of sowing of seed thoughts. It was here at Stockbridge that he wrote works on the freedom of the will, on the nature of virtue, and on original sin, for which he is chiefly noted."[29]

LESSON SEVEN: Revival Testimonies Spark More Revival

The final lesson from the First Great Awakening can be simply stated, "Spread the good report!" Today, more than ever, we must tell the stories of God's move upon the earth. This will help spread the fires of revival. This has been true throughout history. Stories of revival elicit hunger for more revival. These leading revivalists of the First Great Awakening all understood this and were early adopters of spreading the good news in print. As Isaiah 52:7 says:

"How beautiful upon the mountains

are the feet of him who brings good news,

who publishes peace, who brings good news of happiness,

who publishes salvation,

who says to Zion, 'Your God reigns.'"

Paul Dienstberger writes: "When fellow New England clergymen requested letters of explanation about the awakening, Edwards wrote about the events in his *Faithful Narrative of the Surprising Work of God*. The report went through 20 printings by 1738 and was widely read in the colonies and

England. His account contained interviews with those who had experienced changed behaviors. Also, some unusual manifestations began to occur during his sermons with outcries, faintings, and convulsions by those under conviction."[30]

Whitefield: According to author Harry S. Stoudt, "Thanks to widespread dissemination of print media, perhaps half of all colonists eventually heard about, read about, or read something written by Whitefield. He employed print systematically, sending advance men to put up broadsides and distribute handbills announcing his sermons. He also arranged to have his sermons published."[31]

Zinzendorf was also burdened for publishing, noted John R. Weinlick in *Count Zinzendorf*: "It would take several pages to insert only the titles of Zinzendorf's publications, including tracts and periodical works for which he furnished the chief material although they do not bear his name. With the exception of a few smaller tracts in Latin, French, and English, the Count's published works were written in German. Some were elicited by controversies concerning the Moravian churches. However, the greater portion of Zinzendorf's writings consists of sermons, essays, and hymns."[32]

This mighty movement of the First Great Awakening was simply a foretaste of how God uses the stories of revival to whet the appetite of others for revival. The lessons forged in history through Zinzendorf, Whitefield, and Edwards give us hope—hope to believe that God can and will do it again in our day. Their compelling stories give us clear evidence of the pursuits God blesses. When many are saying the church is finished, prayer is not strategic, preaching is outdated, conversion is passé, unity is impossible, missions is irrelevant, and testimonies are sensational, clear historical lessons from the First Great Awakening speak a better word. May we press into these biblical means God uses to forge and sustain revival in those in every generation who will humble themselves, pray, seek His face, and turn from their wicked ways.

CHAPTER 9

THE MOST IMPORTANT LESSONS FROM THE SECOND GREAT AWAKENING

The strangely encouraging fact about the Second Great Awakening is that it began at a time when America was in an unimaginably deplorable spiritual state. The awakening that began at the end of the 1700s and continued through much of the following century is hope-giving because today America finds herself once again in the midst of a spiritual catastrophe. In an article at his website, revival scholar J. Edwin Orr notes the state of America after 1781:

> Drunkenness was epidemic: 300,000 out of 5 million were confirmed drunkards. Women were afraid to go out at night for fear of assault. Bank robberies were a daily occurrence. The Methodists were losing more members than they were gaining. The Baptists had their most wintry season. Most Congregational Churches had not taken in one young person in 16 yrs. The Protestant Episcopal Bishop resigned because he had no work. Chief Justice Marshall said the church was too far gone to be redeemed. Voltaire said Christianity would be forgotten in thirty years. A poll at Harvard revealed not one believer. Princeton discovered only two believers. At Williams College they put on antichristian plays. They burned down Nassau Hall at Princeton. They took the Bible out of local Presbyterian Church and burned it. Christians on college campuses were so few they met in secret like a communist cell, and kept their minutes in code so that no one would know.[33]

As we realize and admit our vast spiritual bankruptcy, we can reach out for a remedy. Jesus taught us that "blessed are those who mourn for they shall be comforted" and "blessed are those who hunger and thirst for righteousness for they shall be filled" (Matt. 5:4, 6). The degree to which we see and repent of our depravity will determine the intensity with which we embrace Jesus. Our hunger for Jesus is linked to our desperation. The biggest downfall of America in this hour is that we are comfortable. But, God is raising up His house of prayer, those who cry out for revival day and night, who are uncomfortable with the status quo. That's where the lesson of the Second Great Awakening comes in: a remnant of believers who gives themselves to praying and working to see transformation can set a country ablaze!

How did the situation change in the United States in the late 1700s? The transformation began with prayer. Two Scottish pastors called the people of their nation to unite in prayer for revival. Jonathan Edwards received a copy of their letter pleading for united prayer for revival. Edwards published *A Humble Attempt To Promote Explicit Agreement and Visible Union of all God's People in Extraordinary Prayer for the Revival of Religion and the Advancement of Christ's Kingdom on Earth, Pursuant to Scripture Promises and Prophecies*. Believe it or not, this was just the title! The book would later launch what became known as "concerts of prayer." Orr summarizes the influence of prayer in this massive awakening in The Awakening of 1792 Onward:

> "The spiritual preparation for a worldwide awakening began in Great Britain seven years before the outpouring of the Spirit there; the believers of one denomination after another, including the evangelical minorities in the Church of England devoted the first Monday evening of each month to pray for revival of religion and extension of Christ's kingdom overseas. This widespread union of prayer covered the United States within ten years and spread to many other countries, the concert of prayer remaining the significant factor in the recurring revivals of religion and the extraordinary out-thrust of missions for full fifty years, so common place it was taken for granted."[34]

Yet for revival to spread beyond the walls of the church, God has to raise up mighty revivalists. These are those who take the fire of the Holy Spirit and spread it to masses of people around the world. During the Second Great Awakening, God raised up many mighty revivalists. I want to focus on just three of them in hopes of inspiring a new generation of revivalists who give their lives to see their cities and nations blazing with Jesus' love. Each of them was greatly influenced by older generations of leaders who imparted the passion to live for the purpose of propagating revival on the earth.

TIMOTHY DWIGHT

As the 1700s came to an end, the fires of revival from the First Great Awakening were long gone. Yet Edwards' experience with revival, writings on revival, and call for prayer for revival would be key in launching another awakening. Once you've tasted revival you are always marked with a hunger for more: this resulted in Edwards' calling the nation to prayer.

One of those Edwards impacted was his grandson Timothy Dwight. He became the president of Yale College in 1795, and used this post to raise up a new generation of revivalists. It was no easy task; seeing breakthroughs in revival never is. Dwight saw that most, if not all of his students were "attached to the deistical fashions of the French Enlightenment," according to Mark Noll, in his book *A History of Christianity in the United States*.[35]

In Dwight's words the students had "infidelity" related to Scripture, leading to unrestrained indulgence. They had embraced the lies of the world rooted in a philosophical spiritualism that rejected the truth of God and His Word. This sounds very much like what we see occurring on our college campuses today. What if God raised up college presidents, pastors, leaders, and parents with the primary agenda of forging a lifestyle of revival in the next generation? That's what Dwight did.

He believed that a "revival of religion" was simply the turning of multitudes in a brief time to feel and confess God's power. He believed that revival was a foreshadowing of the Second Coming of Christ, when Jesus will reign on the earth. Like his grandfather, he believed that only God could send revival. His explanation of revival is quoted in *A God-Sized Vision: Revival Stories That Stretch and Stir.*

> "A farmer may plant the seeds, but rain and sunshine from heaven make the plants grow. So preachers sow the Word, but God alone makes those means effective."[36]

Unlike other Calvinists of his day, Dwight embraced a balanced understanding of the sovereignty of God in bringing revival, and the proper use of means to spark revival. The Bible, prayer, fellowship, catechism, and self-examination were the methods he used tirelessly at Yale to promote revival.

Dwight labored with clear and powerful arguments to restore his students' confidence in the Bible. He preached a four-year cycle of messages on the essentials of the Christian faith rooted in the trustworthiness of the Bible. At the end of four years, he started again at the beginning. He was relentlessly committed to seeing truth conquer the lies believed by his students. In 1801, after seven years of preaching, small sparks of revival began to emerge. It began small and secretly, with a handful of Yale students praying for transformation at their school. God heard their prayers. The following year, one-third of Yale's students proclaimed their faith in Christ. The revival "sent a thrill of joy and thanksgiving far and wide into the hearts of its friends, who had been praying the waters of Salvation might be poured into the fountain from which so many streams were annually sent out," according to *A God-Sized Vision.* "Dwight met with students to pray and hear their confessions. His prayers had been answered, his vision realized as revival spread from student to student....None had seen anything like it, so sudden and so great was the change in individuals. Half of the senior class entered the pastoral ministry."

Read the following accounts of the effects of the Yale revival:

> "One college tutor wrote home to his mom, 'Yale College is a little temple; prayer and praise seem to be the delight of the greater part of the students while those who are still unfeeling are awed with respectful silence." (*The 2nd Great Awakening* by Diane Severance)[37]

> The Yale students learned from their "revival-minded" president. "Those who were privileged to study with Dwight would never forget the courage he demonstrated by directly engaging the moral and intellectual problems Yale's students struggle with as adolescents." (*A God-Sized Vision*)

> "Many of these became agents for revival and reform in New England, upstate New York, and the West...they spread concern for renewal up and down the East Coast. Soon there was hardly a locale in which Christians were not praying for revival or thanking God for having received one." (*A History of Christianity*)

> Freshman Herman Humphrey described the revival as a "mighty rushing wind." He later served as the president of Amherst from 1824 to 1845. Like his mentor, Dwight, he trained his students to seek and discern revival. (*A God-Sized Vision*)

Seasons of revival occurred at Yale again in 1808, 1812-1813, 1815, and 1831: Dwight had smelled the fragrance of revival and would settle for nothing less. He prayed, taught, counseled, argued, and worked with students to bring their hearts to a place of revival. May God once again raise up leaders, old and new, whose primary agenda is to train and release a new generation of revival-minded leaders. Dwight's students, who spread the fires of revival, were his lasting legacy. Haven't the curricula of our current leadership training programs been too short-sighted as we train in methods that fall well short of the goal of seeing revival fill our schools, churches, neighborhoods, cities, and nations? Dwight showed that even in the hardest soil and in the most intellectual environment, God can bring a culture of revival that launches a new generation of revivalists.

FRANCIS ASBURY

The fires of revival were spread in the Second Great Awakening by another second-generation revivalist, Francis Asbury. He was born in England in 1745, and converted at thirteen. Because of abusive treatment by his teacher at school, receiving twenty-four lashes in one day, he quit school that same year and began to spend time in prayer meetings at his house, and to read the journals of Wesley and Whitefield. At sixteen he had a powerful encounter with the Holy Spirit that made him resolve to become a mighty evangelist. At seventeen, he was placed in charge of a Methodist class as a spiritual leader. By eighteen he was a local preacher, and began traveling to towns nearby to preach as often as five times weekly. He followed Wesley's advice to rise at 4 a.m. to pray. He would then go by horseback to visit the poor and diseased, heart breaking for the hurting. By the time he was twenty-one, Asbury had become a pastor under the powerful ministry of John Wesley.

In 1771 he heard Wesley's plea for workers to go to America, so in his early twenties he left his family in England to pursue the transformation of the new land. When Asbury landed in America there were just four Methodist preachers serving three hundred members. When Asbury died in 1816, more than two thousand ministers served a hundred times that many members. That's revival!

Asbury believed that the most effective way to spread the gospel was for those most deeply affected by its power to take it to those most in need of it. He mobilized thousands of ministers, called "itinerants," who would travel constantly, preaching the gospel powerfully and establishing churches feverishly. Noll records how Asbury told his ministers, "Go into every kitchen and shop; address all, aged and young on the salvation of their souls."[38] Before his death, Asbury traveled three hundred thousand miles on horseback, spreading the fire of Jesus across America.

On his first night in America, Asbury attended a church, and on the second night he preached the gospel. Following his first sermon in America, Asbury was greatly impacted upon learning of the sacrifice of a woman who had walked fourteen miles one way, with her child in hand, to hear his message. He said that she was sent to preach to them that night. It was a foreshadowing of the sacrifice he would make to spread the gospel far and wide throughout America. His message to new believers was, "Let us not sleep as others do, but let us watch and be sober." He transformed the vision of ministers in America from a parish mentality to a circuit rider one, a shift that caused the fire of the gospel to fall in small and large communities, and for churches to be planted across the country. Asbury forged ahead in spite of constant illness, weakness, and feet swollen by rheumatism. His food was often the game he hunted as he traveled and cooked on an open campfire. He had so few possessions that everything he owned could fit in his saddlebags. He braved the dangers of wild beasts, horrendous weather, and the threat of Indians—not to mention the little torments of mosquitoes and ticks. At times the pain was so great that Asbury had to be held up by two people so he could preach. On occasions the pain was so intense he was forced to preach sitting down.

Asbury was adamantly opposed to slavery, and met with President George Washington—though to no avail—urging him to sign an emancipation document. The life of a circuit-riding preacher was so rough that half died before the age of thirty. The difficult life of a preacher in the Methodist system caused many to drop out. Asbury urged them, "We must reach every section of America—especially the new frontiers. We must not be afraid of men, devils, wild animals, or disease. Our motto must always be forward."

These circuit-riding preachers were advised to keep the following daily schedule:

1. Wake at 4 a.m.

2. Pray for one hour from 4 a.m. to 5 a.m., and from 5 p.m. to 6 p.m.

3. Read from 6 a.m. to noon, with an hour off to eat breakfast.

Asbury pushed himself to preach once, twice, even three times a day. Stating, "I must ride or die," he read his Bible, prayed, or read commentaries as he rode. He believed that there were three essential components necessary for building an uncompromising church: circuit-riding ministers, quarterly conferences (times of refreshing and reviving for the pastors), and camp meetings (extended Spirit-filled meetings that revived the hearts of the people.) The first camp meeting was at Cane Ridge, Kentucky, an interdenominational gathering that drew thousands. Hundreds were overwhelmed with strange manifestations of God's power. Some fell prostrate. Some got the "jerks." Others screamed out. This was not your ordinary gathering; the Spirit was being poured out. In the next ten years, Asbury led the Methodists to hold more than a thousand camp meetings of their own. Abraham Lincoln's mother was a frequent attendee. By 1811 Asbury was the most well-known person in America.

The years of circuit riding took their toll. Asbury grew weaker and weaker. The book *Heroes of the Holy Life* tells how in 1816 Asbury wrote: "My eyes fail...It is my fifty-fifth year of ministry and forty-fifth of labor in America...But whether health, life, or death, good is the will of the Lord: I will trust

Him; yea, and will praise Him; He is the strength of my heart and my portion forever—Glory! Glory! Glory!"[39]

CHARLES FINNEY

Charles Grandison Finney (1792-1875) launched a new wave of revival in America, leading half a million people to Christ throughout his ministry. According to Noll, "Beyond any doubt, he stands by himself as the crucial figure in white American Evangelicalism after Jonathan Edwards. In fact, a good case can be made that Finney exerted a more significant influence on American life than any other key figure." He adds, "Some argue that Finney should be ranked with Andrew Jackson, Abraham Lincoln and Andrew Carnegie as one of the most important figures in the 19th century...Finney became the mentor to a growing number of ardent young reformers who wanted to see Christianity as they understood it renewing society as well as individuals. Among these reformers were the nation's leading abolitionists."[40]

Finney was the best-known revivalist in the United States. Noll notes that "Finney's range was breath-taking. He created powerful yet controlled revivalistic methods for the frontier (upstate New York, Ohio) and orchestrated successful evangelism in the nation's major cities (Boston and New York City) and in Britain. More than any other he joined evangelical realism to social reform." In *Heroes the Holy Life*, Welsey Duewel claims, "While it is said that 70 percent of the converts even in Moody's meetings became backsliders, it is estimated that 85 percent of the professed converts in the Finney revivals remained true to the Lord."[41]

What were the things that set Finney apart as a modern-day revivalist? Finney lists two "striking characteristics" of the revivals he led:

The first characteristic of Finney's revivals was the prevalence of a mighty Spirit of prevailing prayer. Finney believed that people should not sit back and wait for revival, but should pursue it based upon "the proper use of the means God has given in response to His promises." This shocked many Calvinists in his day, and continues to shock many today. Yet, should we not learn from the call to pray, and the expectation that God will answer? Have we become practical deists in our prayers, as we pray and never expect an answer? That would be absurd to Elijah, who was so sure God would send fire down from heaven that when he challenged the prophets of Baal at Mount Carmel he directed that the altar be filled with floods of water. In Finney's Lectures on Revival, he devotes many chapters to the essential nature of prevailing prayer in revival.

Finney lists eleven characteristics of someone who would commit to prevailing prayer. He:

1. Must pray for a definite object (specific).

2. Must pray in accordance with the revealed will of God.

3. Must pray with submission to the will of God.

4. Must have desire for the object commensurate with its importance (fervency).

5. Must pray with right motives.

6. Must pray by the intercession of the Spirit.

7. Must be persevering in prayer.

8. Must pray a great deal.

9. Must offer prayers in the name of Christ.

10. Must renounce all his sins.

11. Must pray in faith.

Finney's second characteristic of revival was an overwhelming conviction of sin. The chapter "How to Promote Revival" in *Lectures on Revival* is one of the most transforming I've ever read. It is not as simplistic as it sounds. Finney details and urges sincere repentance of twenty-six sins of commission and omission. Hosea 10:12 says:

> "Break up your fallow ground, for it is the time to seek the LORD, that he may come and rain righteousness upon you."

Finney teaches that repentance is necessary to break up the hard ground of our sin-filled hearts, to experience lasting revival. The preaching of repentance is not foreign to Christianity—John the Baptist and Jesus himself began their public ministries with the simple and straightforward message, "Repent!" Many modern believers like myself have greatly benefited from times of repentance resulting from reading this chapter of Finney's. Keith Green, the modern revivalist who died in 1982, was so transformed after reading the chapter that he thought he wasn't saved prior to this experience, and led his entire ministry group to read and repent.

Finney listed sins to repent of to break up the "fallow ground"[42]:

Sins of Omission	Sins of Commission
1. Ingratitude	1. Worldly Mindedness
2. Lack of love for God	2. Pride
3. Neglect of the Bible	3. Envy

4. Unbelief	4. Bitterness
5. Neglect of Prayer	5. Slander
6. Neglect of the means of grace	6. Worldliness
7. Lack of heart/passion in seeking God	7. Lying
8. Lack of love for others	8. Cheating
9. Lack of brokenness over the lost	9. Hypocrisy
10. Lack of godly character at home	10. Robbing God
11. Neglect of service in the community	11. Bad Temper
12. Neglect of watchfulness over your life	12. Hindering others' usefulness
13. Neglect of watchfulness over others	13. Selfishness

Finney called on believers to write down each sin and spend quality time asking God to reveal in depth how they had sinned in each manner, and to write down each transgression. I have gone through this process, and can tell you firsthand that God worked deeply in me as a result. As I was praying for God to forgive me of the specific sin, I received a freeing revelation: repentance isn't simply being sorry for our sin. It is that, but also much more. Repentance is godly sorrow that leads the one repenting to go in a new direction.

Here's an example of the revelation I received—I realized that repenting of a lack of love for God includes both brokenness over the ways I have not loved Him and movement forward to love Him. Repentance involves both repentance from the evil transgression and the glorious movement toward the righteous life. That's true freedom!

CHARACTERISTICS OF REVIVALISTS

As I reflect on the hours I have spent studying and processing the leadership of Dwight, Asbury, and Finney, I am struck with six characteristics they reflected that must be seen in modern-day revivalists as well.

1. They experienced personal revival.

Revivalists must be revived! The depth of passion needed to pursue a life of revival is not forged over a short period of time, but through long seasons with the Lord, and through much perseverance and opposition. Dwight faced failing eyesight and tremendous headaches. Asbury faced horrible physical conditions, illness, and much loneliness. Finney overcame intense opposition from religious leaders of his day, and endured great financial difficulties. The Spirit of God that revives the revivalist does not make the journey easy or smooth, but makes the passion greater as one overcomes each trial. The Bible promises that as we persevere through much opposition, the Holy Spirit will be poured out upon us (Rom. 5:5) and we will overcome by this prevailing love of the Spirit (Rom. 8:37).

As a new generation of revivalists emerges, we must be diligent and consistent in our times with the Lord in order to be filled with His Spirit moment by moment. Only those who experience the reviving of the Spirit daily can then take revival to a broken and fragmented world. If you are like many in this new generation who have yet to have a life-transforming experience with the Spirit, I urge you, like Jacob, to wrestle with God and not let go until He blesses you. The Bible is clear that God loves to give the Holy Spirit to those who ask Him. Like revivalists of old, let's believe that this truth is a sure word for us. Let's ask and expect God to send the outpouring of the Holy Spirit to refresh our souls (Acts 3:19-20). If revival is a new Pentecost, we should, like the disciples of old, shut ourselves up until we receive power from on high. To see the results of the book of Acts, we must be filled with the same Holy Spirit of Acts! God is delighted to pour out His Spirit on those who ask. So ask...and keep on asking!

2. They believed revival would occur.

Dwight was relentless in preaching, praying, and serving the students at Yale until truth triumphed over sin and unbelief. Asbury had no doubt that God would send the fire of His Spirit on the new communities if the ministers would simply go. Even today, Finney's writings inspire people to expect God to move as they obey His Word. It seems in our day that a subtle "intellectual" doubt has dulled the hearts of leaders so that they no longer expect God to do mighty things. Have you heard of the *Built to Last* business book that calls leaders to embrace BHAGs (Big Hairy Audacious Goals)? What about revivalists? Do we believe that God can do "far more abundantly thank all we ask or think, according to the power at work within us" (Eph. 3:20)?

I highly recommend potential revivalists read Mark Batterson's book, *The Circle Maker.* In it he inspiringly calls us to boldly go for big dreams in

God. Have we become so afraid of the "hyper-faith" teaching that we have stopped believing God, not wanting to put Him on the spot? I wonder if the angels and saints in heaven are thinking, "Why are God's leaders so full of doubt about what He can do?"

A new generation of revivalists will sacrifice all their time, money, and energy in pursuit of revival because they know God will do it! I know I will see revival in Austin, Texas before I die. I can't wait to see this amazing city finally fulfill its God-ordained destiny by glorifying Him as the live worship capital of the world, training and sending missionaries worldwide and multiplying 24/7 houses of prayer and outreach. I get fired up just thinking about it!

3. They had one life ambition: the spread of revival.

Finney quit his law practice. Asbury left his family and friends in England to move to America. Dwight shaped his presidency at Yale around the goal of revival. Each of these revivalists made their sole ambition the goal of seeing revival on the earth. I believe God is raising up a new generation of leaders who are living and will die for one cause: to see transforming revival sweep the earth. Any other goal, no matter how noble it may be, is less than the worth and glory that Jesus died and rose again to gain. The earth is the Lord's: Father God created the earth as a reward for His Son. The kingdoms of this world are meant to be the kingdom of our God. We are to contend for God's kingdom to come on earth as it is in heaven. This is the heart-cry of every modern-day revivalist, "This one thing I do: I live to see Jesus exalted by fiery lovers from every tribe and every nation!"

Now is a good time to stop and pray deeply through your life's ambition. What is success? For me, it's nothing less than seeing the city of Austin transformed so that we are sending out thousands of fiery missionaries to bring revival throughout the earth. I have set the course of my life to pursue the goal of revival. Is anything less than that worthy of the holy life that God has given us? Think seriously about pursuing the goal of career, money, happiness, or family. God is mobilizing a radical new generation that loves holiness and loves righteousness. Those who are part of it will not rest until the righteousness of Jesus covers the earth.

4. They trained up the next generation in revival.

Dwight's school, Finney's lectures, and Asbury's mobilization efforts were all focused on reviving the next generation of revivalists. We are short-sighted if we miss the fact that revivals often occur in universities and in young people first. We must embrace the wisdom of these revivalists of old, and pour into a new generation who will carry the passion of revival long after we are in heaven. The passing of the generational pursuit of revival is our responsibility. Do your children know of your passion for revival? How are you focused to impart a passion for God and revival to the next generation? Have you asked God for His strategy for you to leave the legacy and value of the pursuit of transforming revival?

If you are young, you also have a generation below you that you are called to train, love, and lead into passion for Jesus. If you are over forty, like me, you are clearly called to pour into younger men and women a passion for Jesus and the spread of His truth upon the earth. It takes time, effort, and patience to raise up a new generation of revivalists. The Word of God is clear: Paul left us his 1 and 2 Timothy letters to help us train up a new generation. Paul wrote Timothy to guide him in the spread of the gospel in the midst of a hostile land, and that's what we are training the next generation to do. It's time we grow up and see ourselves no longer as consumers, but as transformers who live to see dramatic change in the earth. It begins with the upcoming generation. Let's go for it!

5.   They sacrificed greatly to see revival spread.

Imagine leaving your family at the young age of twenty-one to pursue ministry in a foreign land. Imagine giving up a lucrative law practice to struggle financially in the ministry. Imagine suffering blindness, but never giving up your calling to reach the next generation with revival. Asbury, Finney, and Dwight endured many obstacles to see revival spread in their generation. I love the part in the movie Luther, when his mentor tries to get Martin Luther to back off his radical writings and pursuits. Luther responds, "That day when you sent me out so boldly to change the world, did you really think there wouldn't be a cost?"[43] The same is true today. If you sign on with God's agenda to promote revival upon the earth, you will be maligned, attacked, and ridiculed—often by church people. Not to mention, you will be often hated by a lost world.

As I have studied revival, I've seen that it always comes at great cost. Somebody dies, suffers, is deeply wounded, shot, lied about, or imprisoned in order to fulfill his calling. Paul is a worthy model of suffering for the cause of Christ and the spread of the gospel. He spent years of his life in and out of prison, never giving up despite the hardships. In fact, Paul used his time in prison to write many letters which later became much of the New Testament. Above all, revivalists must not get discouraged by trials. We must expect them and rejoice through them, knowing that the difficulties are not slowing the progress, but are, themselves, gifts of God to prepare us for the spread of revival. Revivalists endure. Revivalists never quit. Revivalists see difficulty as opportunity!

6. They finished well.

Asbury, Finney, and Dwight all fought the good fight and finished the race with hearts and ambition for revival burning strongly until the very end. The secret place of his heart is where a revivalist's character is formed and maintained. Our character is the witness that the revival we seek is truly alive in us. The character Christ forms in us stays steady to the end. He has promised to finish what He's started, to carry us faithfully to the end, and to present us before His throne without spot or wrinkle, and with great joy. Revivalists who finish well must have the long view of life. Never allow unforgiveness, roots of bitterness, offense, or disappointment to cause you to quit. Look around, many are quitting—too many. When we quit, we are showing that it's about us and not about God. He doesn't quit or get nervous, bitter or thrown off. He never gets offended or feels neglected. As upcoming revivalists, we are to be dead to our old nature and alive to Jesus Christ. The old person who gets offended, who doesn't forgive and who gets bitter, is now dead. We are new creatures.

The joy of a revivalist who is finishing well is to say to the next generation: "I've fought the good fight...Now, you fight. I've finished my race...Now, run yours!" Set the course of your life, like those who led the Second Great Awakening, to be a revivalist who finishes well!

Revival Cry

CHAPTER 10

YOUR MOST IMPORTANT PREPARATION FOR THE THIRD GREAT AWAKENING

The coming revival or Third Great Awakening is what I prefer to call a new Pentecost. God is setting up the world for revival by raising up His house of prayer for all nations. The coming revival parallels God's miraculous work in the book of Acts, but will have an even greater, worldwide scope. Acts is a book of revival which sets both the expectations and the paradigm for the upcoming massive awakening. The unfulfilled sections of Acts 2:17-21 reveal a picture of the coming outpouring:

> "'And in the last days it shall be, God declares,
>
> that I will pour out my Spirit on all flesh,
>
> and your sons and your daughters shall prophesy,
>
> and your young men shall see visions,
>
> and your old men shall dream dreams;
>
> even on my male servants and female servants
>
> in those days I will pour out my Spirit, and they shall prophesy.
>
> And I will show wonders in the heavens above
>
> and signs on the earth below,
>
> blood, and fire, and vapor of smoke;
>
> the sun shall be turned to darkness
>
> and the moon to blood,
>
> before the day of the Lord comes, the great and magnificent day.
>
> And it shall come to pass that everyone who calls upon the name of the Lord shall be saved."

Parts of this were fulfilled on the glorious day the church began, but much of it—and I believe the fullness of this promise—will only be seen in the last days' church. We have yet to see the dramatic signs in the heavens; a clear indication that this passage is meant for a future fulfillment. And we've yet to see the Spirit poured out on "all flesh." This is what we are contending for in prayer. In fact, every one of our prayers will find its fulfillment in a coming revival, the thousand-year reign of Christ, and the eternal state when the new heaven and the new earth are the joyous home of God and His children forever.

I believe there are seven key components of the coming revival.

A PRAYER ENGINE

We are living in the most exciting days in human history. We are on the precipice of the greatest move of God ever seen. The "greater works" that Jesus promised in John 14:12 have already been occurring around the world but will be focused in an unprecedented work of awakening before the Second Coming. We will see a mighty fulfillment of Acts 2:21:

> "And it shall come to pass that everyone who calls upon the name of the Lord shall be saved."

What is our part? What are we to do while we wait for this outpouring? Pray! Prayer is the most essential and effective ministry of any believer. God can do more in one second both through us—and even without us—through prayer than through many years of our working in our own strength. The Bible promises that God's work is done "Not by might, nor by power, but by my Spirit says the Lord" (Zech. 4:6). Prayer and outpouring go together like hand and glove. We ask and God fills us with the Spirit (Luke 11:13). This is the source of revival. A growing, supernatural love for God and others comes only and always through a work of the Spirit being poured into our hearts.

The first order of business to prepare and join in the coming revival, then, is to set first things first: prayer. Ministries that have put prayer on the back burner must return to their "first love" and make prayer the driving force, the engine of all they do. Raising up serious and faithful prayer warriors is not a difficult task…it's absolutely impossible apart from the work of the Holy Spirit! The Spirit empowers prayer.

As we look forward to the coming new Pentecost, we must turn our hearts toward prayer as our first vocation. This is a radical departure for most Christian leaders. Yet, this is the model given us by the early church. In Luke 24:48, Jesus told the disciples:

> "You are witnesses of these things. And behold, I am sending the promise of my Father upon you. But stay in the city until you are clothed with power from on high."

The disciples interpreted Jesus' command correctly and responded by "devoting themselves to prayer" (Acts 1:14). Prayer is where we are filled with the Spirit, revived, and empowered to go and take Jesus' love to the world. Imagine a car without an engine; so is the church without prayer. If we are prayer-less, we become power-less, even with great teaching and the most cutting edge strategies. This is a sad snapshot of the modern church in America. But a new day is coming and God's praying church, the house of prayer for all nations, is awakening to the central role of prayer. One of the most enlightening passages explaining this truth is found in Philippians 4:6:

> "Do not be anxious about anything, but *in everything by prayer* and supplication with thanksgiving let your requests be made known to God (emphasis added)."

Do you see that "everything by prayer" is how the church functions in God's economy? In man's system, strategies, leadership methods, church growth plans, programs, and all sorts of good things take center stage. They are good but empty without the engine of prayer which leads to the outpouring of the Holy Spirit.

I experienced a shocking revelation recently. I had just finished my time with the Lord, and having read my Bible and prayed, I got a strange thought. I began to wonder what happened the last few years of Tozer's life, as he became a preaching pastor in Toronto, Canada. I did an online search for "Tozer church," and what I saw astounded me.

Tozer's final pulpit is now one of the largest Hindu temples in Toronto! Shocked is an understatement. God immediately told me that unless I focus on raising up the next generation of leaders, the same thing will happen here at our church in Austin. I immediately began mentoring the next generation with renewed passion: mentoring them in the place of prayer!

Moses mentored Joshua, the next generation leader, by taking him consistently to the "tent of meeting" to be with the Lord. In time, Joshua embraced this calling as his own and remained in the tent long after Moses departed. God is raising up a new Moses generation today—I think of it as those over forty—to mentor the Joshua generation (those under forty) in the place of prayer. In all our leadership strategies have we not missed God's main strategy to raise up leaders in the place of prayer? This prayer engine is the key to passing on revival to the next generation. We must give the Joshua generation a place at the table, and it begins at the prayer table.

My first meeting with three upcoming leaders of the Joshua generation at our church—Zac Tinney, Tyler Schuetze, and Nick Gamez—included an amazing prayer time. As we prayed, God spoke 1 Peter 4:7 to me. I had obviously read it before, because it was underlined in my Bible—but now God was about to underline it in my heart:

"The end of all things is at hand; therefore be self-controlled and sober-minded for the sake of your prayers."

The first part arrested my heart as I remembered that Peter wrote this around 62 or 63 A.D. So, in God's time-line, almost two thousand years ago the "end of all things" was at hand. How much more is it today? Yet, the most impacting part of this passage, the powerful "aha" moment I experienced that day, is the beautiful truth that we are not to allow anything to interfere with that which is most important—our prayers. Paraphrased, the passage says "Jesus is about to return, so be holy and serious-minded so that nothing will mess up what's most important—your prayers!" This is how God views and values His prayer engine. It is key number one in launching and sustaining the coming revival.

A WORLDWIDE SCOPE

Jesus is raising up His house of prayer in the last days to be "a house of prayer for all nations." His heart has always been for all nations. The raising up of Israel as His chosen people was explicitly for the purpose of blessing all nations. God said this clearly to Abram in Genesis 12:2-3:

> "And I will make of you a great nation, and I will bless you and make your name great, so that you will be a blessing. I will bless those who bless you, and him who dishonors you I will curse, and in you all the families of the earth shall be blessed."

Jesus launched His public ministry with a shocking emphasis that caused the Jews to want to kill Him. Surprisingly, Jesus' proclamation that He had just fulfilled the long-awaited Messianic prophecy was not the reason they wanted to kill him. Rather, the account in Luke 4 reveals that it was something rooted in this Messianic calling that infuriated the masses. They raged because Jesus spoke of God's blessing on a Gentile widow and a Gentile army commander. Jesus was fulfilling the Genesis 12 prophecy that He would be a blessing to all nations.

In Acts 1:7-8 Jesus disciples were fixated on the "end-times" calendar, as many are today. Jesus made His priority crystal clear:

> "It is not for you to know times or seasons that the Father has fixed by his own authority. But you will receive power when the Holy Spirit has come upon you, and you will be my witnesses in Jerusalem and in all Judea and Samaria, and to the end of the earth."

The coming revival is a worldwide revival that is prophetically portrayed in the historical events on the day of Pentecost. Relive the events of that amazing day noted in Acts 2:1-13:

> "When the day of Pentecost arrived, they were all together in one place. And suddenly there came from heaven a sound like a mighty rushing wind, and it filled the entire house where they were sitting. And divided tongues as of fire appeared to them and rested on each one of them. And they were all filled with the Holy Spirit and began to speak in other tongues as the Spirit gave them utterance.

> "Now there were dwelling in Jerusalem Jews, devout men from every nation under heaven. And at this sound the multitude came together, and they were bewildered, because each one was hearing them speak in his own language. And they were amazed and astonished, saying, 'Are not all these who are speaking Galileans? And how is it that we hear, each of us in his own native language? Parthia's and Medes and Elamites and residents of Mesopotamia, Judea and Cappadocia, Pontus and Asia, Phrygia and Pamphylia, Egypt and the parts of Libya belonging to Cyrene, and visitors from Rome, both Jews and proselytes, Cretans and Arabians—we hear them telling in our own tongues the mighty works of God.' And all were amazed and perplexed, saying to one another, 'What does this mean?' But others mocking said, 'They are filled with new wine.'"

The prayer meeting overflowed into a revival meeting with worldwide influence. God had ordained that the prayer engine of the new church would from the very beginning launch it into reaching the nations. The heart of God is portrayed from Genesis to Revelation—He loves all nations forever. The coming revival will bring people from various nations together in local congregations, a United Nations of sorts, and will send out believers to cross cultures and learn new languages to spread the good news of Jesus' love. The revived end-times church will be a red, yellow, brown, black, and white church—one body, with no distinctions!

Some of the most promising and inspiring passages on the coming revival are found in the book of Isaiah. It is a book of hope and promise concerning the coming awakening. God has led me to spend close to two years reading, praying about, and learning the promises of revival found there. I just recently learned that one of my favorite, unfulfilled passages was used by Jonathon Edwards to promote united prayer in his day. It's found in Isaiah 2:2-3:

> "It shall come to pass in the latter days

that the mountain of the house of the LORD

shall be established as the highest of the mountains,

and shall be lifted up above the hills;

and all the nations shall flow to it,

and many peoples shall come, and say:

'Come, let us go up to the mountain of the LORD,

to the house of the God of Jacob,

that he may teach us his ways

and that we may walk in his paths.'"

Do you see it? "The nations will flow" to the mountain of the Lord to be taught God's ways and to learn to walk in His paths. That's revival, and it is coming!

A HOLY SPIRIT OUTPOURING

The unique power of the coming revival was promised on the first day of the church, at Pentecost, as noted in Acts 2:17-18:

"'And in the last days it shall be, God declares,

that I will pour out my Spirit on all flesh,

and your sons and your daughters shall prophesy,

and your young men shall see visions,

and your old men shall dream dreams;

even on my male servants and female servants

in those days I will pour out my Spirit, and they shall
prophesy."

The shocking message of this passage is that the final outpouring of God's Spirit will result in widespread, or commonplace, prophecies, dreams, and visions. In other words, the Spirit's manifestations will not be relegated to one section of the body of Christ but will be poured out on "all flesh"— including Baptists, Bible churches, Catholics, Lutherans, Pentecostals, and others. What an astounding day is coming! It's interesting how we can all get locked in by our religious traditions and miss a move of God. Evangelicals often miss the Spirit's move because of doubt, while charismatics miss His move through preconceived ideas of what the gifts will look like. Acts 2 promises that this coming revival won't be an evangelical or charismatic one alone, but will be an "all flesh" revival, meaning that no category of people will be left out. That is staggering and exciting!

Recently two local churches in our city asked to use our facility for some special services. I agreed and decided to attend the meetings. The first night I was blown away as the guest speaker, someone I'd never met, gave a remarkably accurate prophecy about my calling and our church's destiny related to prayer and our facility. It was truly astounding. I played a recording of the prophecy at our service the following Sunday, where people were so encouraged—blown away by the accuracy of the prophecy from a man we'd never met. Yet, as other pastors have experienced, too, soon after I received an anonymous note that said something like this:

> "Pastor, do not get into this supernatural stuff. Stick to preaching the gospel, the Bible, prayer, and outreach."

See what can happen in these last days? We can be offended due to our tradition and miss what the Bible promises us. Prophecy is not a gift for the charismatic brand of the body of Christ. No. Prophecy is a gift for "all flesh," for our "sons and daughters," for "male and female servants." To "stick with the Bible" we must embrace what God promises in these last days. And widespread prophecy is one of the promises that will accompany the new Pentecost, along with increased dreams and visions.

It's time to define our terms. What is the purpose of New Testament prophecy? It's not to give directional words or try to predict someone's future. 1 Corinthians 14:3 gives the clear New Testament purpose for prophesy:

> "The one who prophesies speaks to people for their upbuilding and encouragement and consolation."

The purpose of New Testament prophecy is simply building up another spiritually (for spiritual advancement), encouragement (to reveal God's heart), and consolation (to comfort). Prophecy is a body of Christ blessing that is going to increase in these last days. I've seen it occurring more and more throughout the city church in Austin and found it to be common among evangelicals and charismatics alike. Isn't it amazing that in these last days prophecy will actually be a gift that unites the revived church?

Two clear warnings are needed, however. Prophecies are always subject to the Word of God; they are always to be tested by the Word of God. Prophecies must also be tested by the Spirit's discernment in our hearts. We "prophecy in part," so every word must be tested by the objective Word of God and by internal witness of the Spirit of God. I see it as very rare that God will give a prophecy that isn't conformational. When I receive a prophecy that goes against what I have been hearing from God personally, I put it on the shelf and test it over time. I know for some this is a messy subject, but I've got good news: this gift is from God and it's promised to increase in these last days. If God told you He wanted to give you an amazing gift to build you up, encourage you, and comfort you, would you reject it?

One time in my early days of planting Northwest Fellowship, I was sitting in our office trying to figure out what to do—this is a common dilemma for church planters!—when in walked a man I'd never met. He told me he wanted to connect his missions agency with our church. I told him we were barely surviving, and didn't have much to give at this point. He handed me his group's ministry guidelines. What immediately caught my eye as I read shocked me: "We believe all the gifts of the Spirit ceased with the death of the apostles." I told him I could not agree with that statement. He immediately said that the meeting was over, but asked if he could pray for me. I agreed, because I needed prayer! Then my visitor prayed the most amazing prayer. He "read my mail," obviously led directly by the Spirit to encourage me. After the prayer I thought, "He doesn't believe in the gifts, but he surely flows in them well!"

That day I learned a lesson: functioning in the gifts of the Spirit—yes, even prophecy—can be as natural as breathing, and does not have to be accompanied by any kind of weirdness. It's natural. God flows through His people to encourage, build up, and comfort.

UNLIKELY REVIVALISTS

The most exciting part of the coming new Pentecost is that the move of God will not be focused on one big church, ministry, or ministry leader. This will be a body of Christ revival that will be led by a new generation of those who have been powerfully changed by the power of the Holy Spirit, resulting in a zealous love for Jesus that overflows wherever they go. In the book of Acts, those from the various nations that were at Pentecost went home changed. Many obviously spread the revival in their home towns; they became the first revivalists. The same thing is occurring today. As we have all seen, the day of the super-evangelist who will win our cities and nations to Christ is over. This is the day of the "unknown" revivalists.

In Acts, the apostles were instrumental in leading thousands to Christ in Jerusalem, but it was the rank-and-file believers that became the first revivalists after Pentecost. Acts 8:1 shows the unlikely way God raised up revivalists to move outside Jerusalem:

> "And there arose on that day a great persecution against the church in Jerusalem, and they were all scattered throughout

the regions of Judea and Samaria, except the apostles."

God used another unique method to raise up new world-changers or revivalists, too: He used problems. Yes, problems occur even during revival. The problems experienced by these earliest leaders were the catalysts that led to the choosing of seven servant-leaders to fairly distribute food to the widows. Note that the training ground for the upcoming revivalist is not necessarily in the latest Bible school, or a glamorous internship, but it may be at the place of serving. So be faithful where you are now, and God will raise you up in "due season" to the next place of ministry.

That's what occurred for Stephen and Philip. Stephen progressed from waiting tables to preaching powerfully before the Jewish leaders, becoming the first martyr of the church. Under the Holy Spirit's leading, Philip pioneered new fields by taking the gospel outside of Jerusalem to a non-Jewish audience. God will do the same things in these last days by raising up "non-clergy" types to blaze a new trail for the gospel to new audiences. Are you ready?

Acts also gives us a clear example of the power of unity in the spread of the gospel. Even though they were forging uncharted territories for the cause of Christ, they always worked in unity and in conjunction with the local church leaders or apostles. The enemy would love to bring division in these last days by pitting pastors against non-traditional revivalists. We must work together, pray together, honor one another, and celebrate the work of God through each other. This is a day for unity, a day for power. This is a day for egos to die, and for humility to reign.

This is the day for Jesus to be famous and followed, and for all of us to give all credit to Him. Our ministry titles, our need to be followed, our desire for recognition, the coddling of our insecurities must all die for this coming Pentecost to spread. Humility, dying to ourselves to make much of Jesus, is the overwhelming character trait which must be embraced by revivalists in the next move of God.

PUBLIC MINISTRY

Pentecost did not occur at the Temple—so what if the new Pentecost begins not in the church building but out in the streets? It's a shocking thought for me, as a pastor who spends much of my time building up the body at a church building. But the coming move of God, like the Acts 2 Pentecost, will be in the streets, outside the safety of our church buildings. What occurred in Acts shows the vital importance of "prayer rooms" and prayer meetings that occur in homes and businesses throughout the city. What if the new Pentecost is sovereignly planned to ignite from the prayer meeting you host after work, or in your home? This is the non-traditional nature of the next move of God. God is moving His people out of the building and into the streets, to take Jesus public.

Most of the miracles and salvations that occurred in the book of Acts, if not all, occurred outside the traditional temple or synagogue meetings. God was and is raising up a new strategy. Instead of the church waiting for the world to come to our meetings, we are being sent with love and power to invade the world. It's akin to Joshua leading the Israelites into the land where God promised:

> "Every place that the sole of your foot will tread upon I have given to you, just as I promised to Moses (Josh. 1:3)

We must regain the vision that this new Pentecost is not meant for the church alone, but for the lost who may never enter a local church. That's why you are an essential player as you take revival to your neighborhood, workplace, and city. You are one of the new revivalists who will take Jesus to those in the streets. God is calling pastors to enlist a new army who will go outside the church building to lead a new generation to Christ with an uncompromising message that is shared in shockingly innovative ways. As a believer whose vocation is outside the local church, you are equally called into ministry. In fact, you function now as a missionary to your workplace, neighborhood, and family.

In Acts we see the movement away from the traditional worship in the temple toward a grassroots move of God that establishes His temple in newly transformed communities all over the earth. The church becomes an organic body rather than an organized institution. One of the most encouraging modern-day stories of this grassroots move is noted in the book *Miraculous Movements*, which catalogs the unprecedented move of God among Muslims around the world. The goal is to establish the basic family unit or neighborhood as the church so that it can thrive in the midst of hostility and great persecution. Regardless of how God does it in these last days, He clearly wants to move in the hearts, families, and communities of the world, and establish the grassroots church in once-unreached peoples.

As we've seen from the First and Second Great Awakenings, the church moved out of the box of its building and began to engage the world publicly in preaching, compassion, service, and miracles. Our thinking as it relates to the church today is often Medieval. We view the church as a structure or building in which we can meet together. The coming view of the church is more dynamic, vibrant, life-giving, and community based. Imagine if God moved so powerfully in your neighborhood that it began to function like the church—caring for one another, praying for one another, sharing the gospel, meeting needs. What if your workplace was so powerfully transformed that Jesus rooted Himself as Lord over that community? This is what we are contending for in prayer!

GREAT OPPOSITION

Many wrongly suppose that revival will be unopposed, or will establish some kind of "utopia" on earth. That will occur only in the Millennial reign of Christ. Yet, prior to Jesus' second coming we've been promised a final outpouring of the Spirit resulting in the greatest harvest ever. It will be accompanied by the greatest persecution: Jesus promised us that "they hated me and they will hate you also" (John 15:18). He also warned that in the last days that the love of many would grow cold. That is occurring right now. Do you see that we are in the midst of a great falling away in the church? Be vigilant that you do not fall for the lie of Satan that will manifest in two key ways in the last days—through false teaching and through false liberty.

Satan will deceive "even the elect," if that were possible, by using lies from even respected Bible teachers proposing "man-made" doctrines rooted in immorality. Sex and money will be two key tools the enemy will use to deceive the end-times church. Don't fall for the lie that the pursuit of money and sexual immorality are from God. They are not. The "love of money" and the pursuit of "sexual pleasures" are chief tools of the anti-Christ spirit to steal, kill, and destroy. This satanic strategy is clearly portrayed in the book of Revelation.

Yet, in the midst of this terrible deception, God has a triumphant church that will not bow the knee, no matter the cost. Jesus told us to be prepared to go to jail, to be brought before the courts, to be turned on by our own family members or church members, and to be persecuted unmercifully for His name's sake. Revival will be costly: it always is. But I have gained so much hope as I read two key phrases about being in the midst of the turmoil of the end-time mayhem. Jesus tells His people in Matthew 24:5-6:

> "For many will come in my name, saying, 'I am the Christ,' and they will lead many astray. And you will hear of wars and rumors of wars. See that you are not alarmed, for this must take place, but the end is not yet."

This phrase, "See that you are not alarmed, for this must take place," brings me so much comfort. Don't be alarmed, this must take place. We can't avoid it, but we can overcome it through Christ! The second encouraging word from Jesus is found in Matthew 24:12-14:

"And because lawlessness will be increased, the love of many will grow cold. But the one who endures to the end will be saved. And this gospel of the kingdom will be proclaimed throughout the whole world as a testimony to all nations, and then the end will come."

Jesus promises that in the midst of the great falling away, a remnant of revived believers will be unmoved and full of the fire of God taking "the gospel of the kingdom...throughout the whole world." Do you see what will be occurring in the coming years, and is even beginning today? God has a revived people, whom He calls his house of prayer for all nations, that will spread His love in the midst of the greatest tribulation known upon the earth. This last-days' church will simultaneously be the most victorious one and the most martyred one in history. We will overcome Satan and his persecutions by obeying the clearly defined prescription of Revelation 12:11:

"And they have conquered him (Satan) by the blood of the Lamb and by the word of their testimony, for they loved not their lives even unto death."

Our sure and impenetrable defense against all the fiery darts and rampages of the devil remains the blood of the Lamb, the word of our testimony, and not loving our lives even unto death. Jesus' blood makes us completely righteous. Satan has no ground to accuse us or defeat us. The word of our testimony involves both sharing with others what Jesus is currently doing, and sharing the sure testimony of His Word. The end-times church will also use the final protection like no other time in history; we will die rather than bow our knee to Satan. Death is our final weapon against Satan's onslaught. Since true believers cannot truly die (John 11:25-26), we win by surrendering our earthly bodies to "temporal death," in anticipation of a glorious and triumphal resurrections.

This, obviously, is new thinking for much of the modern "protected church" in America. Virtually no believers living in the United States have ever lost a friend or family member to martyrdom. But that will change in the coming days. Two key scriptures prepare the end-time church for the coming mass martyrdoms:

"Then they were each given a white robe and told to rest a little longer, until the number of their fellow servants should be complete, who were to be killed as they themselves had been (Rev. 6:11)

"And I saw the woman (the great prostitute linked with The Beast), drunk with the blood of the saints, the blood of the martyrs of Jesus" (Rev. 17:6)

Remember Jesus' words and do not be alarmed: these things must take place. We overcome Satan by the blood of the lamb, the word of our testimony, and by not loving our lives to shrink back from death. This is who we are. We are a conquering army, full of love and full of unwavering conviction. We win in life and conquer in death! Through Jesus we are His invincible warriors spreading His love at all costs in these last days. What amazing days in which to be alive!

A THRIVING COMMUNITY

How, you may be asking, will we survive in the midst of the onslaught of evil against the church? One of the key factors to us overcoming is the thriving New Testament community that will be forged during these times of intense tribulation. The Bible urges in Hebrews 3:13:

"But exhort one another every day, as long as it is called 'today,' that none of you may be hardened by the deceitfulness of sin."

And in Hebrews 10:24-25 we read:

"And let us consider how to stir up one another to love and good works, not neglecting to meet together, as is the habit of some, but encouraging one another, and all the more as you see the Day drawing near."

Here we see the power of the encouragement and exhortation of the body of Christ. It functions as both protection and healing. We urge one another daily so that we will not be taken out by the deceitfulness of sin, and we encourage one another daily to stay passionate for Christ and to do good works. The community of Christ is the seedbed of both revival and community transformation. Years ago I heard Willow Creek pastor Bill Hybels say that the church of Jesus Christ is the hope of the world. It's true! Jesus promises to revive us and then send us to bring transformation on the earth. It is essential that we learn to forge healthy and life-giving relationships in the body of Christ. We need each other more than ever.

Are you intimately and intricately connected to the body of Christ? Imagine a thumb or foot trying to survive alone without the rest of the body. It's not possible. Many today, out of fear and insecurity, are trying to function independently of the body of Christ. They are virtually always picked off by Satan's schemes. Get connected and stay connected with God's church!

In the book of Acts we see the Holy Spirit-saturated people of God face all manner of opposition together, victoriously. New communities of Christ, or churches, were formed and the word of God spread rapidly throughout the cities and nations. Revival spread all over the world. You and I today are byproducts of the first Pentecost. Now we are contending in prayer that God will send a final Pentecost to bring in the last harvest. The beautiful thing about living in our day and age is that we have the Bible, from Genesis to Revelation, as our sure road map and a living love letter to guide us triumphantly through every conceivable trial. And truly, I've read the end of the book: we win because Jesus has already won!.

Revival is not a hoped-for dream, but will soon be a living reality. Revival is a promise. We are the house of prayer for all nations, contending day and night for the coming revival. We will never quit. We will never lose. We will persevere through all trials and tribulation, to be presented spotless before His glorious throne. We among all people are most blessed: blessed to live, to contend, to go, to share, to believe, to read, to pray, and to die for Jesus.

Let a Revival Cry begin in your heart, your home, your family, your church, and your city! I'm joining you from Austin, Texas—and together we will see revival with our own eyes before Jesus returns!

NOTES

1. Charismamag.com May 2011

2. JEdwinOrr.com

3. Concordances.org

4. Tozer, AW. *The Knowledge of the Holy*. HarperCollins: San Franciso. 1961

5. Tozer, AW. *The Best of A.W. Tozer*. Christian Publications: Pennsylvania. Pages 109-111

6. Grudem, Wayne. *Systematic Theology: An Introduction To Bible Doctrine*. Zondervan: Grand Rapids

7. Mouw, Richard J. *Abraham Kuyper: A Short and Personal Introduction*. Eerdmans: Grand Rapids. 2011

8. Idleman, Kyle. *Not A Fan: Becoming A Completely Committed Follower of Jesus*. Zondervan. 2011

9. Bound, E.M. *Power Through Prayer*. Whitaker House Publishers. 2005

10. Revival-library.org

11. Watchword.org

12. Dallimore, Arnold A. *George Whitefield*. Crossway: Wheaton. 1990. Pages 42-43

13. Whitefield, George. *Journals*. London: Banner of Truth Trust, 1960. Pages 197

14. Prdienstberger.com

15. Revival-library.org

16. Wheaton.edu

17. *The Moravian Church Miscellany*. J.W. Held. 1853

18. Revival-library.org

19. Prdienstberger.com

20. Dallimore, Arnold A. *George Whitefield*. Crossway: Wheaton. 1990. Page 52

21. Revival-library.org

22. Prdienstberger.com

23. Sermonillustration.com

24. Patheos.com

25. Movements.net

26. Revival-library.org

27. Revival-library.org

28. DesiringGod.org

29. GreatAwakeningdocumentary.com

30. Prdienstberger.com

31. Digitalpuritan.net

32. CountZinzendorf.ccws.org

33. JEdwinOrr.com

34. J. Edwin Orr. The Awakening of 1792 Onward. JEdwinOrr.com

35. Noll, Mark A. *A History of Christianity In The United States and Canada.* Eerdmans: Grand Rapids. 1992. Page 168

36. Hansen, Collin. *A God Sized Vision: Revival Stories That Stretch And Stir.* Zondervan: Grand Rapids. 2010

37. Christianity.com

38. Noll, Page 171

39. Duewel, Wesley. *Heroes of the Holy Life.* Zondervan: Grand Rapids. 2002

40. Noll, Pages 176-177

41. Duewel, Page 92

42. Finney, Charles G. *Lectures On Revivals Of Religion.* E.J. Goodrich: Oberlin, Ohio. 2005. Pages 34-42

43. imdb.com

ABOUT THE AUTHOR

Trey started Northwest Fellowship in 1993 and has been in full-time ministry since 1986. He has a Masters of Divinity from Oral Roberts University and did Doctor of Ministry work at Fuller Seminary. His passion is Jesus and his beautiful wife Mary Anne and two amazing daughters Lindsay and Christina!

In 2009 God led Trey to launch the Unceasing Prayer Initiative where 40 churches have been praying 24/7 ever since for unity and revival in Austin, Texas! You may contact Trey Kent for more information or speaking requests at trey@northwestfellowship.com or follow him on twitter @trey_kent.

Made in the USA
Columbia, SC
02 November 2019